ENCYCLOPEDIA OF

Scary things

enter if you dare

Written by Barbara Cox and Scott Forbes

Idea by Ariana Klepac

Sandy Creek
NEW YORK

CONTENTS

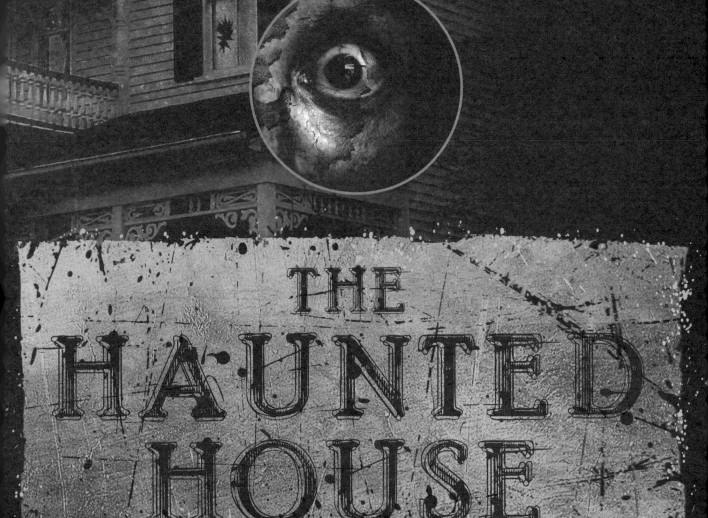

THE
HAUNTED
HOUSE

GHOST

GHOST

OTHER NAMES: Phantom, specter, wraith, spirit, spook, revenant, apparition.

FACT OR FICTION: Scientists say fiction, but many people would claim otherwise.

DESCRIPTION: Often a very pale, almost transparent version of the living person. Sometimes invisible. However, some ghosts look like ordinary people. Can be surrounded by extremely cold air. May shriek, sigh, or moan. Animals can also have ghosts.

WHERE THEY LIVE: Anywhere, such as old houses, castles, dark alleyways, theaters, stations, airfields, country roads, ruins, forests, and lakes.

POWERS: Can appear or disappear at will and may continue to haunt a place for hundreds of years, seeming indifferent to the passage of time. Can cause extreme fear if they want to.

WEAKNESSES: Ghosts have a problem with salt—they don't like to cross it or touch it in any way.

DIET: Ghosts do not need to eat or drink.

OTHER CHARACTERISTICS: May be associated with a violent death, and appear every year on the anniversary of the killing. Certain places seem to attract ghosts and are known for hauntings.

A GHOST can appear after a person has died. Many ghosts are not scary at all, others are quite terrifying, but they're all mysterious. Nobody knows why they appear. If someone was murdered or died horribly in some way, after death they might come back to wreak revenge.

THE APPEARANCE OF GHOSTS

Phantoms, specters, and wraiths, which are the most frequently seen forms of ghosts, are pale grey or white in color, and misty. They seem to float in the air and you may be able to see right through them. Some ghosts can't be seen at all, but can only be felt as freezing cold air, especially if you walk through them! There may be a surrounding sense of dread, or just a feeling that someone else is there.

The ghost of someone who was executed by beheading may walk around carrying his or her own severed head. A murder weapon may still be visible, such as a knife in their ghostly back. Other phantoms might display bloodied clothes or terrible wounds.

There are numerous stories of ghosts who appear to be a normal living person, until they suddenly disappear, walk through a closed door or solid wall, or perform some other supernatural act.

MYRTLES PLANTATION, LOUISIANA, USA

Built in 1796, this house is said to be haunted by numerous ghosts. Supposedly, up to ten people have been murdered there, so it's not surprising. Ghosts of two little children have been seen playing on the veranda. Someone's last dying steps can be heard climbing the stairs. In one room where a soldier was killed, there is a body-sized blood stain which cannot be removed by any method. The ghosts of several slaves who met unfortunate deaths sometimes appear to ask if chores need doing. The grand piano plays by itself— just one haunting chord over and over again. One story claims that the spirits of a mother and her children are contained in a large mirror.

HAUNTINGS

If the ghost is someone who was murdered or died horribly, he or she is probably still angry about it. But sometimes they just seem to be fond of a particular place and decide to come back and haunt it.

Many ghosts seem to be stuck in a pattern that they have to repeat. For example, they always cross a certain room, or look out of a particular window, or walk up a flight of stairs—sometimes the stairs are no longer there and the ghost climbs up in mid-air. These ghosts usually ignore people and may walk straight through them, which apparently feels very strange if you're the person being walked through.

Other more malicious ghosts don't want to share their favorite place and go around scaring off any living people who try to move in by terrorizing them with screams.

WARNING GHOSTS

Some ghosts are only seen when they show themselves in order to warn the living of a forthcoming event, usually a death in the family. Legend is that at Arundel Castle in Sussex, England, a white owl always appears when one of the family is going to die.

Other ghosts, more usefully, have been able to stop accidents, especially on train tracks, mountains, or roads—they appear at the place where they were killed themselves, and warn the living to be more careful. These often look like ordinary people and witnesses may not realize there was anything strange about them until later.

ANIMALS AND GHOSTS

Ghosts of various animals have been seen, including those of dogs, cats, horses, deer, sheep, owls, and chickens. Living animals are also well known for being aware of ghosts. People first realize that there's a supernatural presence because their dog growls or snarls, apparently at thin air. Horses especially dislike ghosts, but cats seem to be less concerned.

There are tales of ghost hounds terrorizing travelers at night on lonely roads.

APPARITIONS

There are many cases of people having an unexpected vision of a relative, loved one, or friend, often someone who is far away, and then finding out later that the person died at exactly that moment. These ghosts usually seem very normal and are not distressed at all; they only appear once to give the news of their death and are not seen again. This kind of ghost may be called an apparition. (See also Doppelgänger on page 182.)

BERKELEY SQUARE

There is a terrifying ghost story attached to the address 50 Berkeley Square in London, England. The ghost of a madman is said to haunt the top bedroom of the house. If anyone spends the night in that room, it is said they will wake up either dead or insane.

GHOSTS IN FAMOUS PLACES

The Capitol Building in Washington DC, USA, is said to be haunted by several murdered politicians and two workmen who died while building its dome.

The ghost of Abraham Lincoln is said to haunt both the White House and Ford's Theater where he was assassinated.

The Château of Blois in France houses the ghost of a former Count of Blois. He fights against a ghostly enemy, in an endless duel, which has been going on since the sixteenth century.

Windsor Castle, home of the British royal family, has several royal ghosts, including Queen Elizabeth I and her mother Anne Boleyn, who runs down a long corridor while screaming.

The Tower of London, where the King's enemies used to be imprisoned before being put to death, is the most haunted building in Britain. The best known of its many ghosts is Margaret Pole, the Countess of Salisbury, who was executed in 1541 at age 71.

Top: The ghost of Queen Elizabeth I appears to England's Queen Victoria at Windsor Castle.

COMMUNICATING WITH GHOSTS

A séance is a meeting of a group of people who try to get in touch with ghosts. They may use a ouija board, which is a board with the letters of the alphabet marked on it so that a ghost can spell out a message.

A medium is a living person who can communicate with the dead. In the nineteenth century, there was great interest in the afterlife, and people paid mediums large sums of money so that they could hear messages from their dead relatives, or see a loved one's ghost.

A medium and her guests attempt to communicate with the dead.

GHOSTS AROUND THE WORLD

Ghosts are known in every country in the world and there are different customs for dealing with them.

Countries in Asia have a Ghost Festival, which may last as long as a month. This is a time when ghosts are free to roam the land of the living and must be taken care of. In China, special attention is paid to hungry ghosts—the unhappy ones. It's important to make sure that these ghosts find their way back to Hell at the end of the festival.

The Day of the Dead in Mexico and other parts of Latin America is a time when people remember their dead relatives and friends and encourage them to come back and visit. Flowers are left for them and food is put out, on graves and in homes. The atmosphere is joyful, to welcome the ghosts, and motifs of skeletons and skulls are used as decorations.

Most of Europe has a tradition of remembering the dead on All Saints' Day and All Souls' Day (November 1 and 2), and in several countries a meal is left out and the house is kept warm for any ghosts who may visit at this time. (See also Halloween on pages 102–107.)

WHITE LADIES

There are many stories of pale ghostly women who haunt country roads or other remote places. They are usually the ghost of a local girl who was murdered, or had her heart broken and then committed suicide. Some White Ladies simply wail and moan, but many are angry at their fate and will try to lure passing men to their doom. Some haunt lonely bridges, such as the one in France who stops any man who tries to cross over and asks him to dance with her. If he refuses, she grabs him with terrifying strength and throws him down into the rushing river below.

Top left: The ghost of Okiku, a Japanese girl who was thrown down a well by her master for breaking a plate.
Left: Mexican decorated skull.

THE PHANTOM HITCH-HIKER — A MODERN WHITE LADY

O n a deserted highway late at night, a solitary driver stopped to pick up a beautiful girl hitch-hiker. She sat quietly in the car and didn't say much. When they reached her destination, the driver looked around to see that she had vanished. Later, he learned that a girl died tragically near the same stretch of road.

Above and right: White Ladies are ghosts of broken-hearted women wishing to wreak revenge on living men.

POLTERGEIST

Above: Poltergeists are mischievous spirits that cause havoc in a house.

IF NO ONE CAN BE SEEN, but plates are thrown across the room, there's hammering on walls and floors in the middle of the night, and heavy furniture moves by itself, you might have a mischievous Poltergeist in your house.

MISCHIEVOUS SPIRIT

Unlike ghosts, which often show no interest in the people living in the house they are haunting, Poltergeists are definitely hostile to the human occupants. They deliberately break treasured objects, wait for them to be replaced, and then break them again.

Poltergeists continually make sudden loud noises so that nobody can relax. They especially like to stop human beings from sleeping, and may even bite, pinch, or hit them to keep them awake. Life with a Poltergeist soon becomes intolerable.

Often, when the exhausted family moves out, the Poltergeist disappears and will not trouble the next occupants at all. Families afflicted by a Poltergeist almost always include teenagers. Some believe that Poltergeists are drawn to the energy given off by a restless, and perhaps unhappy, child.

The Bogeyman is going to get you!

NIGHT MARE

A spirit that sits on your chest while you are asleep and gives you bad dreams.

In Scandinavia, the Night Mare is a female spirit called the Mara. She rides horses at night, leaving them mysteriously exhausted the next morning. In Germany, the Night Mare is male and is a kind of goblin called an Alp or a Trud. It gets in through the keyhole. In Japan, nightmares are brought by a monster called the Baku.

BOGEYMAN

The Bogeyman is a legend invented by parents to make small children behave.

The Bogeyman is a traditional scary figure which parents use to threaten their children, telling them that "the Bogeyman will get you if you leave the house alone/pick your nose/torture the neighbor's dog" or whatever it may be. The Bogeyman is made as scary as possible by adults. Often he has long skinny arms for grabbing children, and he carries a sack on his back for taking the naughty ones away. The Bogeyman exists in every country and in every language.

YAKKA

An ugly Sri Lankan house demon which can cause disease and other troubles.

A Yakka is small, dark, and so incredibly hideous that you really don't want to look at it—meeting its gaze could make you very ill. If you annoy a Yakka it could even make you mad. Yakkas are believed to be the causes for almost all illnesses and accidents that happen around the home in Sri Lanka.

BOGGART

A nasty, hairy creature that lives in houses and can make people's lives miserable.

A Boggart is similar to a Poltergeist; it also likes to destroy houses, but there are some differences. A Boggart is usually visible, being described as short, hairy, and smelly. Moving houses will not solve anything if you have a Boggart—it always stays with the family it has decided to torture, so it will simply move with you.

Most Boggarts are found in the north of England, where they may live under a bridge while they wait for a new family to torment.

Hanging a horseshoe on the door of the house is said to keep Boggarts away.

CHANGELING

IF A CHILD wakes up one day and seems to have gone through a personality transformation, it might be a Changeling that has been left in place of the human child that was stolen by fairies during the night.

SUBSTITUTE CHILD

Sometimes, other beings—usually fairies, but also elves or trolls—decide to steal a human baby and raise it themselves. They take the baby and leave another child in its place. This is called a Changeling.

Sometimes the Changeling is not even a fairy child, but a substitute made by using magic out of a twig, in which case it will soon get sick and die. Changeling children that do survive are often strange-looking, difficult to manage, bad-tempered, and not affectionate—though they are usually smart.

It seems fairies like to steal a human baby that is attractive to look at. In Ireland it was once considered dangerous to compliment a mother loudly about how cute her baby was, in case the fairies should hear.

Changelings will probably just leave their human family one day, and go back to their own kind, but it's very unlikely that the human child will ever come back.

THE
FOREST

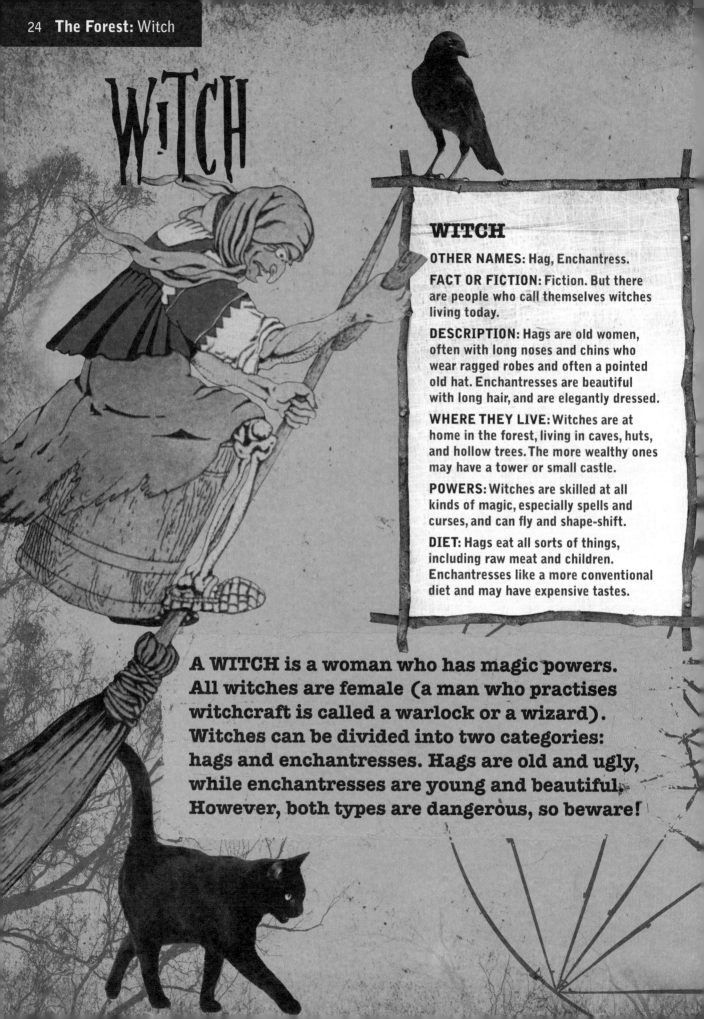

WITCH

WITCH

OTHER NAMES: Hag, Enchantress.

FACT OR FICTION: Fiction. But there are people who call themselves witches living today.

DESCRIPTION: Hags are old women, often with long noses and chins who wear ragged robes and often a pointed old hat. Enchantresses are beautiful with long hair, and are elegantly dressed.

WHERE THEY LIVE: Witches are at home in the forest, living in caves, huts, and hollow trees. The more wealthy ones may have a tower or small castle.

POWERS: Witches are skilled at all kinds of magic, especially spells and curses, and can fly and shape-shift.

DIET: Hags eat all sorts of things, including raw meat and children. Enchantresses like a more conventional diet and may have expensive tastes.

A WITCH is a woman who has magic powers. All witches are female (a man who practises witchcraft is called a warlock or a wizard). Witches can be divided into two categories: hags and enchantresses. Hags are old and ugly, while enchantresses are young and beautiful. However, both types are dangerous, so beware!

BE WITCHED!

Witches are famous for casting spells. They have a great store of magic knowledge, which they can use to do anything from summoning up the spirits of the dead to turning naughty little boys into toads. Not all of their magic is harmful—they're capable of healing and doing good, but they have plenty of magic weapons at their command if anyone should annoy them. Enchantresses can become very fond of human men and will cast some unpleasant curses if they're rejected by them.

Almost all witches can shape-shift (turn themselves into something else) if they want to. They may prowl through the forest in the form of a large wildcat or a she-wolf, or fly through the night skies as a bird of prey. Witches can also learn things about distant or future events by gazing into a mirror or a crystal ball (this is called "scrying")—though other people can do this too and not all fortune-tellers are witches!

WITCHES' SABBATH

The Witches' Sabbath is the name given to the nocturnal meetings of a group of witches, where they get into all sorts of evil things! Although called the Sabbath it can take place on any day of the week.

BUBBLE BUBBLE TOIL AND TROUBLE

Witches' spells are often made in the form of a "potion" or magic drink—one that may seem normal and even delicious, but a few sips of which can have an unexpected effect, turning the drinker into a tree-stump, donkey, stone, centipede, or anything else the witch's warped sense of humor has devised. For this reason it is very unwise either to upset a witch or, if you should happen to find one at home, to have a drink with her. Traditionally the potions are brewed in a huge, round metal pot called a cauldron.

GRIMOIRES

This is a kind of witches' handbook. Inside it is all kinds of information, from details about how a witch should dress, what tools to use and how to make them and, of course, spells. There are charms, incantations, and rituals to follow. There are some actual grimoires still in existence from the Middle Ages, from people who called themselves sorcerers.

FLY WITCH FLY

All witches can fly. They use a variety of things to fly in or on, from a forked wand or spade to an airborne bicycle. In ancient Greece and Rome the power of flight was always associated with witchcraft. Witches would either transform themselves into birds to fly, or they might fly on the backs of animals. But by far the most popular flying aid is a broomstick. It must be an old-fashioned broom known as a besom, which has a bundle of twigs tied to a wooden handle. Riding this, a witch can fly far and fast, making her extremely hard to catch and therefore safe from enemies. Witches will fly long distances to attend meetings with other witches, called "covens."

WICCA

Not all witchcraft is evil. In recent times a certain type of "magic" has become popular again, called Wicca (the word is taken from the Old English word for "wise"). This kind of witchcraft is considered helpful, and its followers believe that they can solve problems and cure diseases using various spells and potions that are based on ancient traditions. There are even shops in major cities that sell the ingredients needed—from dragon's blood powder and devil's shoestring, to special mixes that are said to attract love or money, or create a peaceful home.

WITCH DOCTORS

A witch doctor is a very different thing from a witch. A witch doctor is someone living in tribal cultures of Africa, Central America, and the Caribbean, who practices magic as part of the tribe's religion. The term "witch doctor" is very old-fashioned, and today we would call these people medicine men or shamen.

These medicine men use their magical powers for healing, telling the future, or protecting the tribe from, or getting rid of, evil spirits. (See also Voodoo on page 178.)

MORGAN LE FAY

Morgan le Fay, or Morgana, might look beautiful but don't be fooled—she was a nasty piece of work and caused her half-brother, King Arthur of Camelot, endless problems. In some stories Morgan was an evil fairy ("le Fay" means "the fairy"), while others have it that she was just a wicked human with magical powers, specializing in the black arts that some say she learned from the great wizard Merlin.

Always on the look-out for a handsome knight to bewitch, Morgan took a particular liking to Sir Lancelot, who unfortunately was already in love with Queen Guinevere. Although she was her lady in waiting, Morgan was jealous of Guinevere, and began to hate her with a passion. She decided to tell King Arthur about Guinevere and Lancelot.

She made a magical horn from which only "honest" women could drink, in order to expose the cheating Guinevere. Morgan also stole Arthur's famous sword, Excalibur, and sent it to Arthur's enemy in a desperate attempt to overthrow him.

THE FAMILIAR

Every witch has a Familiar. This is a spirit that takes the form of an animal—usually a black cat; a bird such as a crow, owl, or magpie; or sometimes even a toad, rat, mouse, squirrel, or spider. The Familiar is the witch's companion, but it's much more than a pet. As a powerful spirit, it helps the witch to perform magic spells and rites, and protects her against enemies. Sometimes the Familiar is more magically powerful than the witch herself. Familiars often have strange names. Some famous fictional Familiars have been called Pyewacket, Vinegar Tom, and Grizzel Greediguts.

For centuries, people were suspicious of any black cat in case it was a witch's Familiar, but in fact there was no need to worry about this, since most black cats have absolutely no magical ability whatever. If you ever meet a black cat which genuinely is a witch's Familiar, you'll know because your hair will stand on end and you'll feel very uncomfortable.

A few centuries ago, witch-hunters would often need no more proof that a woman was a witch than the fact that she lived alone and owned a pet cat, bird, or mouse!

QUEEN ANNE BOLEYN

Anne Boleyn, second wife of King Henry VIII of England from 1533–36, was believed by some people to be a witch because she had six fingers on one hand and a lump on her neck. These were thought to be typical signs that a woman was a witch. The gossip was that she had taken the King away from his first wife by casting spells on him. This was really all part of a plot to enable Henry to get rid of her and marry someone else.

Below: Not all witches were ugly old hags who lived in hovels. There were thought to be witches among the rich and powerful, too.

WITCHES' HATS

Witches supposedly wear tall, black, pointed hats. However, very old stories and legends about witches don't usually mention witches wearing hats. During the time of the Salem Witch Trials in seventeenth-century America, tall pointed hats happened to be the fashion of the time, so that might be why witches have been shown wearing hats like that ever since.

BABA YAGA

Baba Yaga was an old and ugly Russian witch who liked to eat people (especially children). She flew around in a huge magic mortar steering it with the pestle and sweeping up the wind with her witch's broom to help her fly faster. Baba Yaga was best known for her house, which could be found deep in the forest. It stood on chicken legs and feet and could run through the trees screeching horribly, but come back to its permanent place in a yard closed in by a fence of bones with skulls along the top.

TESTS TO IDENTIFY A WITCH

For a long time, roughly between the fifteenth and eighteenth centuries, people throughout Europe (and later in North America) believed that witches were living amongst them and were plotting to destroy the Christian Church. Many ordinary women (and some men) were accused of being witches and were forced to go through tests to prove their innocence.

They would be:

- Examined for marks on their bodies
- Deprived of sleep
- Tortured to make them confess, using the rack or thumbscrew
- Burned, as it was believed that a witch could not heal from a burn
- Dunked in water because it was believed that a witch would always float. If they were proved to be witches they would be burned at the stake.

WITCH HUNTS

At different times in history people have become afraid of the power of witches and have tried to hunt them all down and destroy them. This unfortunately led to people who were not witches being accused of witchcraft and often unfairly tortured and even killed.

From medieval times until the seventeenth century, certain men took it upon themselves to become official witch hunters. In 1644 a man in England named Matthew Hopkins supposedly discovered his first six witches in Essex. After this he was named Witch Finder General, and he proceeded to cause havoc, accusing women all over the place of practicing witchcraft. Generally he would force a confession from the innocent women and then they would be hanged.

In 1692 in the small town of Salem, Massachusetts in the USA, two young girls began to behave strangely and a number of adults were accused of bewitching them. Soon almost everyone in the town was accusing each other of witchcraft, and a series of trials took place. Twenty-three people were found guilty and imprisoned or even executed. Either there was a freakishly high population of witches in Salem or someone made a very big mistake and many innocent people lost their lives.

CIRCE

Circe was a mythical Greek enchantress who lived in a forest. She was very beautiful, but could be cruel and vengeful, especially to men who rejected her. She was an expert poisoner and was famous for turning anyone who annoyed her into an animal or bird. The most famous story about Circe is where a band of Greeks led by Odysseus were on their long journey to get home after the Trojan War. They arrived at Circe's palace, and she entertained them, but the men annoyed her and she gave them a potion that turned them into pigs. Only Odysseus was still in human shape as the god Hermes had given him a special herb to protect him. He pleaded with Circe to transform the pig-men back, and in the end she agreed, but only if they stayed with her for a year and a day.

KRAMPUS

A hairy, horned figure feared throughout the European Alps, Krampus follows St. Nicholas, or Santa Claus, as he makes his rounds at Christmas. While Santa hands out presents to good children, Krampus punishes the bad with his birch whip and carries off the truly wicked to devour in his lair. (But don't worry, the Krampus only takes away the VERY worst behaved children, and that's definitely not you!)

LESHY

If you go down to the Russian woods and hear whistles, claps, and laughter, or even the voice of a friend (how weird!), it might be a Leshy, trying to lure you off the path and trick you into losing your way. Local people describe this forest spirit as human-like, though he may have a tail, wings, fur, and glowing eyes, and can change size at will. Their advice for warding him off is to make the sign of the cross, throw a bronze button at him, or try to make him laugh.

BONNACON

A bull-like creature with the mane of a horse, the Bonnacon is said to live in southeastern Europe and western Asia. Its horns pose no threat, since they curl back around its head. But if it turns its back on you, watch out, for it can blast out a spray of stinking, burning dung that will cover everything in sight!

BANSHEE

THE MOURNFUL WAILING of this female spirit is one of the most feared sounds in all of Ireland. Drifting out of the depths of the night, it is said to predict the death of a member of the family that hears it.

VOICE OF DOOM

Banshees are more often heard than seen, but they are known to assume different human forms. Some appear as horrible old hags, while others are beautiful damsels with long fair hair and flowing gowns. Their songs, too, vary, from enchanting sad laments to high-pitched screeches that can shatter glass.

The name of the Banshee comes from the Irish Gaelic words "bean sidhe," meaning "woman of the fairies." Ancient legends say that fairy women came to the funerals of members of the greatest Irish families to sing a song for the deceased. Being in touch with the supernatural world, these fairies would know of the death as soon as or even before it happened, and would appear as if by magic.

Similar spirits are thought to dwell in other Celtic realms. In Wales, the Witch of Rhibyn brings news of death to the oldest Welsh families, while in Scotland the call of the Bean Nighe, or Little Washerwoman, strikes terror into the hearts of highlanders.

WINDIGO

AMONG THE NATIVE AMERICAN peoples of eastern North America, few figures of legend arouse more fear than the Windigo, a terrifying giant of the forests with a taste for human flesh.

BLOODCURDLING HOWL

You're more likely to encounter the Windigo (also called Wendigo or Weendigo) in winter, when food is scarcer and it wanders widely in search of prey, mainly at night. You might hear its bloodcurdling howls drifting through the snowy woods after dark, and detect its stomach-churning stench. Few people have seen one and lived to tell the tale, but their reports suggest it resembles either a hulking, hairy ape-man, or a fearsome Zombie with grey skin and its flesh in tatters.

It's said that a Windigo is born when a lost traveler goes so long without food that he or she starts to crave human flesh, or a person is bitten by a Windigo or overtaken by its spirit. A sudden desire to eat other humans is a sign of such possession and would cause Native Americans to leave their communities or commit suicide to avoid harming others. The only way to destroy a Windigo is to burn it, since its heart is a block of ice and must be reduced to a puddle before it will die.

MNGWA

Many otherwise fearless hunters who regularly track down lions and leopards in Tanzania, east Africa, live in terror of the Mngwa, or "strange one," a giant cat bigger than a lion or a leopard and even fiercer. As large as a donkey with thick, grey, striped fur, it is mentioned in old African songs and was reported to have claimed several human victims in the 1920s and 1930s. The victims, who had been totally mutilated, were said to be clutching grey hairs in their dead hands. Europeans who heard the stories of the Mngwa assumed that it might be a dragon, rather than a cat-like creature. There have been many unsuccessful attempts to hunt and kill the Mngwa.

BOKWUS

If you stroll through a spruce forest in northwestern North America and catch sight of a painted face peering at you through the trees, beware. For it could be a Bokwus, an evil spirit of Native American lore that hunts human souls. Its favorite trick is to sneak up on people fishing and throw them under the water to drown them.

ASANBOSAM

In the forests of Ghana, Côte d'Ivoire, and Togo in west Africa, danger may lurk on high. Human-like vampires called Asanbosams are said to hang from branches by hooks at the ends of their legs, ready to snatch up or drop onto passersby and tear at their throats with teeth made of iron. The mere mention of the name is supposed to bring bad luck—so never say it out loud!

WEREWOLF

WEREWOLF

OTHER NAMES: Wolfman, lycanthrope, loup-garou (French).

FACT OR FICTION: Fiction.

DESCRIPTION: Normally human but they change into a wolf at night, at a full moon, or whenever they want to.

WHERE THEY LIVE: Anywhere as humans, though mainly forests when in wolf form.

POWERS: Very strong, often larger than normal wolves.

WEAKNESSES: Can be repelled with the herbs wolfsbane, rye, and mistletoe. Can be injured with silver weapons and killed with a silver bullet.

DIET: When in human form it eats normal human food, but as a werewolf it eats what a wolf eats (any kind of meat!), or it might not eat at all.

FAMOUS WEREWOLVES: The Beast of Gévaudan; Gilles Garnier (a French hermit who confessed to being a werewolf and having eaten four children in 1573); Peter Stumpp (the Werewolf of Bedburg, Germany, who killed 18 people in the mid-1500s).

A WEREWOLF is a human being who changes into a wolf. Some people are born werewolves, others become werewolves later in life as a result of a curse being laid on them or as a punishment for some wrongdoing. There is no known cure.

CURSE OF THE WEREWOLF

There are a few theories as to why people become werewolves. Two sure-fire ways are to be bitten by a werewolf or to be cursed by a sorcerer. Some people choose to become werewolves and rub a magic ointment on themselves or put on a bewitched wolf skin belt in order to transform. A couple of other rather unpleasant ways are to drink the rainwater that gathers in the footprint of a werewolf or to drink water from a cup fashioned from the skull of a werewolf.

THE WEREWOLF LOOK

Werewolves turn into wolves at night and are usually bigger and fiercer than a real wolf, with red, glowing eyes. They may run around on all fours or walk on two legs. Either way, they are horrifying, since they spend most of their time using their huge claws and fangs to attack and devour animals, people, and even bodies from graveyards.

By day, however, a werewolf will normally return to human form and may appear quite normal—aside from some telltale signs. If you suspect someone of being a werewolf, check whether they display any of the following: eyebrows that meet in the middle, particularly hairy skin or hairy palms, pointed ears, a stumpy tail, unpleasant body odor, or a dislike of bright light. If so, be on your guard. Another sign is hair inside the skin, but that's a lot harder to check!

BY THE LIGHT OF THE MOON

Some werewolves can change into a wolf whenever they wish, others have no control over their condition and may find themselves turning into a wolf every time darkness falls, or, more usually, whenever there is a full moon. Often the werewolf will wake in human form the next day, with no recollection of the awful things they have done.

THE BEAST OF GÉVAUDAN

Between 1764 and 1767, the village of Gévaudan in central France was terrorized and more than 100 people were said to have been killed by a huge wolf-like beast that walked on two legs. The French king sent troops to hunt the beast and eventually it was killed. Descriptions of its body vary, but it was said to be very strange and have small ears and hoof-like feet.

Above: The Beast of Gévaudan.

THEY'RE EVERYWHERE!

Stories of werewolves come from all over the world and date back thousands of years. In ancient Greece, wolfmen were mythical figures associated with the gods and there were shrines and cults devoted to them. Ancient Romans believed that magic spells and herbs could turn a person into a wolf— a "versipellis" or "turnskin" they called it. In eighth-century Iraq, scholars reported that wolf-like monsters killed hundreds of people and stole children from their beds.

By the Middle Ages, belief in werewolves was widespread in Europe, but people had come to think of them as the servants of the Devil. So werewolves were greatly feared and people with wolf-like tendencies were persecuted. This was particularly the case in sixteenth-century France, where suspected werewolves were regularly burned alive.

STOPPED IN ITS TRACKS?

A silver bullet can stop a werewolf in its tracks and even kill it, but that might not be the end of your troubles. For it is said that unless their bodies are burned, werewolves return to life—as vampires!

NAVAJO SKINWALKER

In the southwestern United States, people don't just turn into wolves but also coyotes, bears, cougars, and foxes. The people in question are Navajo Skinwalkers, medicine men who supposedly have the power to transform themselves into animals simply by wearing their pelts. Their Navajo name, "yee naaldlooshii," means "with it, he goes on all fours." If that's not alarming enough,

Skinwalkers don't just frolic around, playing at being animals—they use their new powers to attack, maim, and kill their human enemies. They can also take over people's bodies just by looking them in the eye. The only way to stop a Skinwalker, it is said, is to shoot it with a bullet dipped in white ash.

LYCANTHROPY

Feeling a bit bristly? Canine teeth getting bigger? Hungry? Could be a touch of lycanthropy. That's the scientific term for a medical condition that causes people to think they are turning into a wolf or other dangerous animal. It was common in medieval times, and cases still occur.

IMP

According to legend, Imps were among the followers of Satan, or the Devil, thrown out of Heaven by God.

Since then, Imps have often found favor as servants of witches or wizards, though many wander alone. As demons go, Imps are usually small in size and more mischievous than evil. Nevertheless, they can be quite alarming in appearance, having thin, scaly, lizard-like bodies, pointy ears and noses, and bat-like wings. Their tricks can be rather unpleasant, too. Some of their favorites include tripping people so that they hurt themselves and tricking people into getting lost, especially in forests.

EVIL FAIRY

In general, the small supernatural beings known as fairies are good and friendly toward humans. But you can't trust them all.

Some fairies have turned evil and will do all they can to cause terror and suffering. They place curses on people to make them sick or bring them bad luck. And they steal people's souls—even those of babies—and hide them away. In place of the stolen soul, they leave behind a "changeling," an evil or mad creature that will terrorize and torment its new family. In Ireland and Scotland, where such fairies are common, people who seem troubled or distracted are often said to be "away with the fairies."

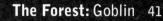

GOBLIN

GOBLINS ARE SMALL supernatural creatures who pester, infuriate, and even terrorize humans. Descriptions of them vary, though they are usually said to be human-like, child-sized or smaller, sometimes bald, and often green in color, with a pointed nose and ears and an almost constantly sly expression.

LITTLE ROGUES

The word goblin comes from the Greek "kobalos," meaning rogue. These little guys are certainly mischievous, as well as frightening and sometimes downright evil. Normally they live in forest caves or tree hollows, but they often take up residence in houses, mainly with the aim of driving the human occupants crazy. To achieve this, they steal things, make strange noises, move furniture around, clatter pots and pans, and rap on walls. So, if you hear any bumps in the night, it could very well be a goblin.

Some say that goblins emerged in the British Isles and then spread across Europe. But similar creatures have been known for centuries in many parts of the world, including India, China, and Japan. Particular kinds of goblins have also emerged within Europe, including the Kobolds of Germany, which create havoc in silver mines, and the Trows of Scotland's Orkney Islands, which live in earth mounds and sneak into houses at night to work their mischief.

Goblins are often very small, some no higher than a few centimeters tall.

WILD MAN

FABLED IN MANY PARTS of Europe in particular, the Wild Man is a huge human-like creature, covered in thick hair, who lives in dense forests. He is sometimes referred to as the Wodewose, an Old English term meaning "wild person of the woods."

WILD AND HAIRY

Wild Men seek out the most inaccessible forest realms, living on nuts, berries, and the raw flesh of animals, and sometimes sleeping in caves. They have no desire to mix with normal humans and can become violent if they encounter them—occasionally they even attack and eat people. Especially savage are the Wild Men of the Alps, who have legs as thick as tree trunks and will immediately tear to pieces anybody who has the misfortune to wander into their domain.

Forest beings like the Wild Man are described in ancient literature. The Greek historian Herodotus claimed to have seen them in North Africa in the fifth century BC, and Greek myths include similar figures such as the Silvanus, the wild protector of the woods, who occasionally punished humans. In the Middle Ages, the Wild Man became a famous figure of folklore in Europe and was often depicted in paintings, coats of arms, and carved into the architecture of great buildings, such as Canterbury Cathedral in England.

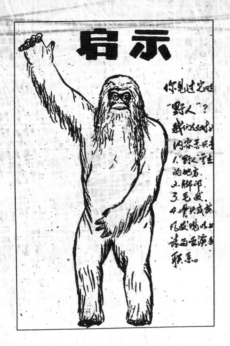

CHINESE WILDMAN

Many travelers roaming the forested hills of the Hubei region of central China have had the fright of their lives when coming upon the Chinese Wildman, also known as the Yeren or Man-Monkey. Described as being 9 ft (3 m) tall, powerfully built, and covered in reddish hair, he is thought by some to be a Chinese ogre, though others say he might be a species of human-like ape, or a giant orangutan.

MO-MO

Also known as the Missouri monster, Mo-mo was first seen in the woods near the town of Louisiana, Missouri, USA, in 1972, by two girls on a picnic, and later sighted repeatedly in the region. A hairy, human-like ape more

than 6½ ft (2 m) tall, it is thought to feed on dogs and other animals. Most people are struck by its foul smell—"worse than a family of skunks," said the first witnesses.

GOATMAN

In Prince George's County, Maryland, USA, this frightening beast with the legs and hooves of a goat and the upper body of a human—and some say horns and pointed ears—is said to roam the countryside attacking cars with an axe. One theory is that he was formerly a scientist working in a nearby research laboratory whose experiment went disastrously wrong, turning him into the Goatman.

JERSEY DEVIL

In January 1909, a huge flying creature with bat-like wings, a reptilian body, and a horse's head and hooves scared the wits out of people in southern New Jersey, USA. According to numerous reports, it swooped over buildings, attacked a bus, left hoofprints in the snow, and was fired at by police. Though it has been seen rarely since, a reward was offered for its capture in 1960 and many believe it still haunts the pinewoods.

ORANG PENDEK

Venture into the remote forests of Sumatra in Indonesia and you might bump into this alarming apelike human trudging through

the trees. Powerfully built and about 3–5 ft (1–1.5 m) tall, the Orang Pendek has long been part of local folklore but has also been sighted by scientists. Some say it's a member of a lost tribe of prehistoric humans, others an undiscovered species of ape.

Left: Jersey Devil.
Above right: Orang Pendek.

NANDI BEAR

It sounds kind of cute, doesn't it? But the Nandi Bear, a fierce meat-eating mammal said to inhabit the forests of western Kenya in Africa, doesn't just savage its victims, it also likes to feast on their brains—in fact one of its nicknames is "brain eater." The Nandi is unlikely to be a bear, since there are no native bears in Africa, but could be an overgrown form of hyena or, some say, a prehistoric carnivore previously thought to be extinct.

Cornish Owlman

Two young girls on vacation at the village of Mawnan in Cornwall, England, in April 1976, reported seeing a human-sized owl, with pointed ears, red eyes, and massive, pincer-like claws hovering over a church. They were so scared that their family decided to return home. Sightings occurred regularly over the next two years and have been reported occasionally since. The sightings coincided with some strange weather patterns that were going on (alternating heat waves and cold snaps) and an increase in the appearance of UFOs.

Beast of Bodmin Moor

Since 1983, more than 60 people claim to have seen a massive, black panther-like creature roaming Bodmin Moor in Cornwall, England. Many have heard its terrible howls drifting across the fields and some claim their animals have been slain by it. Photographs and videos of the creature have been taken, but attempts by scientists and even soldiers to trap it have all failed.

Beast of Exmoor

A great cat-like creature is also said to roam Exmoor in Devon and Somerset, England, attacking sheep and cattle and posing a threat to walkers. It was first reported in the 1970s and near-panic set in during the 1980s when a farmer claimed the beast had killed more than 100 of his sheep by ripping out their throats. Said to be as large as a panther, the beast has a grey or black coat and can leap over fences 6½ ft (2 m) high.

THE
SWAMP

HINKYPUNK

THE HINKYPUNK, also known as Will o' the Wisp or Jack o'Lantern, is a marsh spirit whose treacherous light draws travelers to a swampy death.

BEWARE OF THE LIGHTS

Hinkypunks are found all over the world, wherever there are deserted and dangerous marshes, bogs, and swamps.

The Hinkypunk crosses the marsh, carrying a light which, from a distance, looks like a lantern or torch carried by a human traveler. People who are lost in the marsh follow the light in the hope of finding a way through, but the Hinkypunk leads them astray and they step into the deep watery mud, never to be seen again.

Hinkypunks go around the marshes alone or in groups—the groups are more dangerous, since they usually spread out along a "path," and their lights look as if a row of people are walking safely through the swamp.

Some believe that a Hinkypunk only has one leg, which it hops on nimbly. This would account for the typical bobbing movement of the light. In fact, it is not known what a Hinkypunk looks like from close up, since nobody who has gotten close to one has ever come back to give a description.

GRINDYLOW

A Grindylow is an unpleasant creature that lives in deep ponds and swamps.

A Grindylow likes to live at the bottom of a deep, still pond or a swamp, preferably somewhere where the surface of the water is covered with weeds so that it's very hard for people to see where the bank ends and the water begins. If you should accidentally step into the water, the Grindylow will grab you with its long skinny arms and drag you down into the depths, where it will probably eat you. The best-known Grindylow is Jenny Greenteeth,

who has lived in various marshes in the West of England and is said to be responsible for the disappearance of a number of children.

GRENDEL AND HIS MOTHER

The Anglo-Saxon poem *Beowulf*, written in the tenth century, tells how the King of the Danes and his people were continually being attacked by Grendel, a giant monster who lived under the swamp. Grendel often attacked when the Danes were feasting, since he hated to hear people singing and having a good time. The brave fighter Beowulf battled with Grendel and finally defeated him, ripping off Grendel's huge arm. But Grendel's mother came looking for revenge, and was even bigger and much, much nastier than her son.

MOKÉLE-MBÊMBE

The Mokéle-Mbêmbe is said to live in the swamps of the Congo River in Africa. It's a big greyish-creature with a long neck, a small head, and a long tail. Some say that it looks like a dinosaur. It's not known to be dangerous, but it would probably be alarming if you met it suddenly. It may be a living reptile—some type of lizard, or even a dinosaur which has somehow survived—or it may be a kind of river spirit.

BEHEMOTH

The Behemoth is an enormous swamp-dwelling monster mentioned in the Bible (Book of Job, Chapter 40). Not much is known about it except that it is very, very large. It may be like a hippopotamus, only much bigger. People often refer to huge things today as "Behemoths."

Top: Behemoth is a massive hippopotamus-like creature that is mentioned in the Bible.

MANTICORE

The Manticore is a terrifying man-eating monster from ancient Persia and India.

This legendary monster is famous for devouring every part of its victims, including their clothing and any luggage they might be carrying. If you are eaten by a Manticore there will be nothing left behind at all, not even your shoelaces!

The Manticore lives in jungles and swampy areas in India and ancient Persia (now Iran). It has the body and legs of a lion, the head of a man with piercing blue eyes, three rows of teeth, and a long tail with a sting at the end and detachable poisonous spines. As the monster waves its tail angrily, the deadly spines

whizz through the air toward you. If they hit you they will probably kill you. The Manticore can run extremely fast and has an ear-splittingly loud voice that can paralyze victims with fear, giving it plenty of time to pounce.

There's not much chance of survival if you do meet a Manticore. If you can really think on your feet, it may be possible to bide some time by asking it a clever riddle, but it will have heard most of the good ones since it's been around for a very long time. (See also Sphinx, page 170.)

STYMPHALIAN BIRDS

The mythical hero Hercules had to get rid of the ferocious and poisonous birds that were living in the swampy Lake Stymphalia. These birds had metal beaks and feathers. They could pull out their feathers and throw them like poison darts. They ate people as well as crops and fruit, and terrorized the neighborhood. Hercules shot most of them with arrows, after which the remaining birds moved elsewhere.

HYDRA

THE HYDRA is a many-headed serpent which is extremely dangerous and very hard to kill. The Hydra appears in tales of ancient Greece, but there are Hydra legends from Africa too.

POISONOUS BREATH

The Hydra is like a huge water-snake, but has many heads, usually nine. One problem with a Hydra is that if you cut off one head, two more will grow in its place. Only one of its heads, if cut off, will actually kill the monster, and there's no way of telling which head that is. Another problem is that the Hydra has extremely poisonous breath, so you're likely to be dead before you've cut off more than one head anyway, just by letting the monster breathe on you.

HERCULES AND THE HYDRA

Hercules managed to kill a Hydra, but with help. He got his nephew Iolaus to scorch the stump of each head the moment Hercules had cut it off to stop the heads from re-growing. The main head proved hard to hack off with a sword so Hercules had to smash it with a rock. Despite wearing cloths over their mouths, Hercules and Iolaus were almost killed by the Hydra's poisonous breath before it was defeated.

LIZARD MAN OF SCAPE ORE SWAMP

A strong human-like creature with lizard skin.

The Lizard Man has been seen since the late 1980s around Scape Ore Swamp in North Carolina, USA. It is tall, and mostly covered in greenish-black hair but with lizard-like skin on its hands, feet, and face. It has three toes on each foot and three fingers on each hand, is very strong, and has done damage to cars, which it seems to dislike.

HONEY ISLAND SWAMP MONSTER

An ape-man of the Louisiana swamps.

This monster has been sighted since the 1960s. It's a human-like creature, about 6½ ft (2m) tall, with long greyish hair and red eyes. It smells disgusting, and its footprints have only four toes. Honey Island Swamp is a very wild area along the Pearl River in Louisiana, USA. At least 13 people there have claimed to have seen the monster, and, apparently, there are others who prefer not to say in public if they've seen it or not, but privately admit that they have met "the thing," as it's locally known.

Lizard Man of
Scape Ore Swamp

THE
MOUNTAIN

DRAGON

DRAGON

OTHER NAMES: Firedrake, Draco.

FACT OR FICTION: Fiction (probably).

DESCRIPTION: Very big, immensely strong reptilian creatures, with long claws and scaly skin which may look metallic. Most have leathery bat-like wings. Some have several heads. Some are longer and more snake-like in shape. Can be any color, but green and coppery-brown are the most common.

WHERE THEY LIVE: Caves, mountains, rivers, in remote areas. Can take up residence near a village and gradually consume all the inhabitants and their livestock before moving on.

POWERS: Many dragons can breathe fire or toxic fumes. Some can shape-shift into human form. All are highly intelligent, ruthless, and often cruel. They can read the minds of humans.

WEAKNESSES: Vain, may be susceptible to flattery.

DIET: Meat, preferably still alive. Cattle (eaten whole), people, especially young girls. Fire-breathing dragons are thought to need sulphur in their diet.

OTHER CHARACTERISTICS: Live to a great age and acquire mystic knowledge and wisdom. Many are fond of treasure.

DRAGONS are huge, mythical flying reptiles, fire-breathing or water-dwelling, and they are powerful and dangerous. Dragons of different types are found all over the world. Since many dragons love treasure, they can often be found guarding it. If you want to soothe a dragon, give it gold or jewels.

HERE BE DRAGONS

It's often believed that ancient maps used to have the inscription "Here Be Dragons" (in Latin, "hic sunt dracones") in unexplored areas. In fact, only one known map has this inscription: the Hunt-Lenox Globe, which dates from about 1505 AD. The area it marks as dragon-infested is in eastern China.

TYPES OF DRAGON

Many different descriptions of dragons have come from different countries, but they can all be classified into two main types: fiery dragons and watery dragons.

Fiery dragons: These are most often found in western legends and histories. They are the dragons that breathe fire and destroy towns and villages by flying over and scorching them. They're fierce, proud, and cruel, and are the enemies of humans.

Watery dragons: These are more common in Asian countries. They're longer and more snaky than the fiery dragons, and are closely linked to water. Sometimes a watery dragon can be the spirit of a river or mountain stream, and will suffer if the stream dries up or is polluted. This type is much kinder to humans, though they still need to be treated with great respect. Watery dragons may appear in human form.

Below: Sigurd killing the dragon, Fafnir.

LEGEND OF FAFNIR

In Scandinavian mythology, Fafnir had to guard a priceless treasure. But he became so obsessed with it that he turned into a greedy and dangerous dragon. He was killed by the hero Sigurd (also known as Siegfried). After being splashed with the dragon's blood, Sigurd finds that he can now understand the language of birds. He hears the birds talking about a plot to kill him, and therefore is able to defeat his enemy.

DRAGONS AND TREASURE

Fiery dragons are very fond of gold and jewels. Over their long lives, they collect vast amounts of treasure, which they hide in mountain caves. One dragon may take over a treasure when another one dies, so some hoards are very ancient. Dragons are well aware that treasure is attractive to humans, and may use it as bait, allowing unwary thieves to wander into the cave and to stare in astonishment at the riches on display. The dragon may even chat with them for a while, before eating them. It is unwise to join any expedition to steal a dragon's hoard.

ORIENTAL DRAGONS

Dragons are important in Asian culture, especially in China, Vietnam, and Japan.

Here is a list of some Chinese dragons, together with a description of their temperament and powers.

Shenlong is a rain dragon, with shining blue scales. If annoyed, it can cause thunderstorms and hurricanes.

Tianlong is the celestial dragon, another sky-colored Chinese dragon that has power over clouds.

Fucanglong is a fiery dragon that mostly lives underground and guards treasure and mineral wealth in the earth. A volcano erupting is thought to be the Fucanglong bursting angrily out of the mountain-top.

Ch'i is a mountain dragon, tricky and easily annoyed.

Jiaolong is a dragon of floods and rivers. It can shape-shift into a number of different forms including people and fish.

A VENGEFUL DRAGON

Kiyohime was a pretty young girl who was an innkeeper's daughter. One day she fell madly in love with a young Buddhist priest. However, the priest thought that she wasn't good enough for him because he was educated and she was just a lowly maid. When he rejected her, Kiyohime wanted revenge. She studied magic and learned how to turn herself into a dragon. In her dragon shape, she tracked down the arrogant young man and killed him.

Ee dente vortiget   sum doluisset impetii sect m

THE RED DRAGON
OF WALES

The national emblem of Wales has always been a red dragon. This goes back to an ancient story about Merlin, the great wizard.

The story tells how a red and a white dragon had been fighting each other and doing terrible damage to the country. They were captured by magic and imprisoned under the hill called Dinas Emrys.

All was quiet then for centuries, until King Vortigern tried to build a castle on the hill. Each day the workmen would start building the walls, and each morning they would find that their work from the day before had been destroyed during the night. Local wise men led Vortigern to a young boy called Merlin, who lived near the hill and who was known to have magic powers. Merlin told the King about the dragons under the hill. Nobody believed him, but finally Vortigern had the hill opened up. Everyone was terrified as the two huge dragons flew out and at once began fighting again. A battle followed, and at last the red dragon overcame and killed the white dragon. This was the beginning of Merlin's career as a great wizard.

Top: Battle of the red and white dragons.
Left: The red dragon of Wales.

St. George And The Dragon

St. George, who was originally an ordinary Roman soldier, was once journeying through a desert land when he came to a town where a dragon had taken over the only source of water.

In order to get any water to drink, the people of the town had to give the dragon food, to persuade it to move away from the water for a while each day. At first they had fed it with sheep, and then, when the sheep ran out, the dragon had indicated that it would be more cooperative if it was fed with young girls. The girls from the town were being eaten one by one, and were drawing lots to see who would go next.

The King's daughter had drawn the fatal lot, and although her father wanted to overrule the result, she insisted that it was her turn and she would go to be eaten like all the other girls. The King had promised all kinds of treasure to anyone who would send their own daughter to the dragon instead, but no one had offered.

Fortunately, at this point St. George arrived. Protecting himself with the sign of the cross, after a hard fight, he killed the dragon with his spear, and the King's daughter was saved.

St. George slays the dragon, saving the King's daughter from a horrible death.

Medusa, one of the three Gorgon sisters.

GORGON

THE GORGONS of ancient Greece looked like women but their hands were made of brass, they had long claws and long sharp teeth, and instead of hair their heads were covered in live snakes. Their stare would turn you to stone.

SERPENTINE SISTERS

The Gorgons were three sisters: Stheno, Euryale, and Medusa. Stheno and Euryale were immortal, but Medusa, the youngest, was mortal. The Greek hero Perseus succeeded in killing Medusa, with the help of several gods (Hermes lent him some winged sandals, Hades lent him a hat of invisibility, and Athena lent him a brightly polished shield). Moving swiftly in the sandals, and unseen by Medusa because of the hat, Perseus was able to use the shield like a mirror and see where the Gorgon was without looking at her directly, so he could kill her without being turned to stone. He cut off her head, which lost none of its power. He used it to defeat several enemies before he presented it to the goddess Athena, who kept it on her shield.

PERSEVS·SHOWING·THE·GORGON'S·HEAD·

BURU BURU

The Buru Buru is a legendary giant lizard from the most remote valleys in the Himalayas. It is bigger than a Komodo dragon; which is the biggest lizard. The Buru is over 20 ft (7 m) long. It is dark blue in color and has three rows of spines down its back. Not much is known about its character or habits, but if it's anything like the Komodo dragon, they will be pretty unpleasant.

MINHOCÃO

The Minhocão is like a huge black version of a garden earthworm: some reports have described it as 80 ft (25 m) long, with two tentacles or stalks on its head—these may be its eyes, like those of a snail. It is so powerful that it can uproot whole trees in its path and is covered with bones that create a kind of armor for its body. It is said to burrow through the earth in unexplored parts of the highlands in South America.

Right: The Buru Buru resembles the Komodo dragon.

TAZELWURM

The Tazelwurm or "worm with feet" has been sighted in the Swiss, Bavarian, and Austrian Alps. It is described as whitish and lizard-like but smooth-skinned and not scaly. Its head is shaped more like that of a cat, and the worm is about 8 ft (2.5 m) long. Its bite is said to be poisonous and it leaps extremely well. It protects itself by having very tough skin that a knife or sword cannot penetrate. If a Tazelwurm is injured, you can see that its blood is green. It is also known as Bergstutzen (mountain stump), Springewurm (jumping worm), or Stollenwurm (tunnel worm).

BIGFOOT

A KIND OF APE-MAN seen in remote areas of North America. Some say he looks like a tall, light brown gorilla but that he stands upright like a human and makes a strange whistling noise. He is very shy, so it is mostly only Bigfoot's giant footsteps in the snow that are seen by people.

BIGFOOT

OTHER NAMES: Sasquatch.

FACT OR FICTION: Most people think that Bigfoot is fact, since footprints have been found. Some famous scientists believe in its existence.

DESCRIPTION: Like a tall, hairy gorilla or ape-man, but standing upright like a human. Some say Bigfoot has short, light-colored fur or hair all over while other say dark or red hair. Around 6–10 ft (2–3 m) tall and probably weighs more than 500 lb (230 kg).

WHERE THEY LIVE: Remote forest areas of the Pacific Northwest region of North America in Canada and the United States. Bigfoot is thought to be nocturnal.

POWERS: Physically huge and powerfully built, so it can easily catch and overpower large animals or humans.

WEAKNESSES: Does not like bright lights or daylight. Shy of humans.

DIET: An omnivore, meaning that it eats both meat and plants.

SIGHTINGS OF BIGFOOT

The first reported Bigfoot was seen in the Pacific Northwest of North America. Hunters reported meeting a very tall, hairy figure in the mountains, looking like a light-brown gorilla but standing upright like a human. The creature was shy, and when anyone approached, it would disappear into the forest. Its footprints were seen in the soft mud along rivers and were up to 2 ft (60 cm) long. It made a strange whistling noise. The Native American Lummi Nation had many stories about this creature, and it was also known as the Sasquatch, based on the name it had amongst the First Nation people over the border in Canada.

Later, people in the Great Lakes area, and then in some southeastern states, began saying that they had seen a Bigfoot in their own part of the country. There were numerous sightings in California, and reports have come from many parts of the USA over the years.

Bigfoot mostly seems to be wary of people and not dangerous, unless you do something to harm it. However, some people believe that seeing it will bring extremely bad luck. (See also Yeti on page 66.)

ATTACK OF THE BIGFOOT

In 1924, five men mining for gold in the wild Mount St. Helens area of Washington state saw huge footprints and heard strange whistling sounds which seemed to call and answer each other across the valley. As they were coming back to the cabin, two of the men saw a Bigfoot some distance away. They fired their rifles at it, and were sure they had wounded it before it disappeared into the forest. That night, the men awoke from their sleep in terror. The cabin was being attacked by a group of Bigfoot. One got its huge arm through a gap in the wall and tried to grab an axe that was hanging there, but the miners shot at its hand and it pulled its arm back. Luckily, the cabin was strongly built and the Bigfoot weren't able to get in.

Hunters in the snow come across the terrifying sight of Bigfoot.

YETI

A MYSTERIOUS ape-like creature of the Himalayan Mountains, also known as the Abominable Snowman. It is a large, two-legged creature, covered in long hair. Like Bigfoot it is tall and walks like a human, rather than an ape, and leaves large footprints.

YETI

OTHER NAMES: Abominable Snowman.

FACT OR FICTION: Some people believe it is fact, especially people living in the Himalayas, but most scientists think the Yeti is fiction.

DESCRIPTION: An ape-like creature covered in long hair, which walks on two legs like a human.

WHERE THEY LIVE: Mountains in the Himalayan region of Nepal in Asia.

POWERS: Strong and physically powerful. But it may only attack to protect itself.

WEAKNESSES: Shy of humans, so rarely seen.

DIET: Unknown.

ABOMINABLE FOOTPRINTS

The main evidence for the Yeti, or Abominable Snowman, is the large footprints in the snow, which have been seen quite often. Some scientists believe that in certain weather conditions, footprints will spread in snow and give the impression of a much larger foot than they were actually made by; so they think the prints could be made by a bear or even a fox.

However, Yeti have been seen by local Tibetan people. For example, one girl was herding yaks when a Yeti appeared and grabbed her. Luckily, it let her go when she screamed loudly, but the monster killed two of her yaks.

Several expeditions have gone to the Himalayas trying to find evidence of Yeti, but without success. All the same, many people believe that Yeti do exist.

SAVED BY A YETI

In 1938, Captain d'Auvergne, who was the Curator of the Victoria Memorial in Calcutta (Kolkata), India, and a highly respected scholar, was traveling alone in the Himalayas. He became ill with snow-blindness—a condition resulting from over-exposure of the eyes to ultra-violet light; it causes sudden loss of sight and acute pain. He wandered blindly in the mountains until he was close to dying from exposure to the elements.

Then, suddenly, he was rescued by someone, carried to a cave, and fed. As his sight gradually returned, he saw that his rescuer was a tall and hairy Yeti, which gently nursed him back to health until he was well enough to go home.

OTHER YETI-LIKE CREATURES

There are similar stories told all over the world, of hairy ape-men living in the wilderness. Most of these creatures are from mountainous areas.

Yeti-type creatures have also been seen in Queensland, Victoria and New South Wales, Australia. In the Basque country of Northern Spain, the creature a similar creature is known as the Basajaun. In Vietnam, Laos, and Borneo there is a creature called the Batutut, and in South America there is one is called the Maricoxi. For something that supposedly doesn't exist, it turns up in a lot of places!

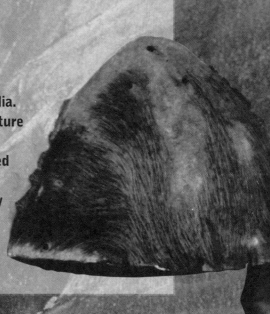

Right: A preserved skull, said to be that of the Yeti, is on display at a monastery near Mt. Everest.

GIANT

GONZAGA II

GIANT

OTHER NAMES: Colossus, Titan, Goliath.

FACT OR FICTION: Both. (Real-life giants are ordinary people who simply grow much taller than normal. We are only talking about mythical giants here!)

DESCRIPTION: Very big people.

WHERE THEY LIVE: Anywhere.

POWERS: Legendary giants are immensely strong, and some have magical powers.

WEAKNESSES: Few, since they are generally huge and untouchable.

DIET: Normal human diet, but in very large quantities. May eat humans.

OTHER CHARACTERISTICS: May live in castles or huge mansions.

Above: The mythical one-eyed giant and Cyclops, Polyphemus.

A GIANT is like a human being but much, much bigger. There are legends of giants from all around the world, but generally they are enormous in height and incredibly strong. Some giants are kind and friendly but others can be terrifying and even eat humans.

WERE GIANTS HERE FIRST?

The ancient Greeks believed that the first beings on earth were the Titans, who were both giants and gods. The Titans were defeated by the "Olympian" gods and disappeared from the world. The gods took over, led by Zeus, and ruled the world from Mount Olympus. But the giants, who were descended from the Titans, rebelled and made many attempts to seize power back from the gods. These giants were believed to be still around in the early days of humankind.

Some Native American tribes of North America have similar beliefs, telling how the early human beings had to battle against human-eating giants who were the enemies of the Great Spirits.

Indian Hindu tradition tells of the Daityas, power-hungry giants who fought against the Devas (gods). Many different peoples around the world have legends that giants lived before today's smaller people arrived.

Some tales of giants may have been created to explain the existence of large ruins that were in fact remains of earlier human civilizations. Some unusual rock formations were explained by saying that giants must have moved the rocks. But for whatever reason, different societies all over the world have the same belief that giants once walked the earth before we did.

PAUL BUNYAN

A legendary American giant and lumberjack.

It's said that when Paul Bunyan was born, it took five storks to bring the baby since he was so enormous.

Paul Bunyan is credited with creating several famous American landmarks. Legend says that he dug the Grand Canyon with his axe. Also, his pet ox, Babe, was so massive that it needed a bigger place to drink, so Paul Bunyan dug out the Great Lakes. Another story tells that the 10,000 Lakes of Minnesota were formed from Paul's footprints and Babe's hoofprints as they once walked together through a great snowstorm.

FINN MCCOOL

An Irish giant who created the Isle of Man.

Finn McCool dug out a clump of earth and threw it at another giant. The clump landed in the Irish sea and formed the Isle of Man, while the hole where the clump had been became a huge lake. He wanted some stepping stones to make it easier to get from Ireland to Scotland, so he built the Giant's Causeway, a huge platform of rock columns reaching into the sea.

a cloak of invisibility, a cap of knowledge, and swift-moving shoes. With these magic tools, Jack is able to outwit the Devil himself and free a captive lady, who marries King Arthur's son.

Jack continues on his giant-killing career, exterminating another two-headed giant named Thunderdel and then finally the giant Galigantus, who has a whole crowd of knights and ladies in captivity, including a lady who has been turned into a white deer by evil magic. Jack frees them all and, once the giant is dead, the lady resumes her true form. Jack marries her, is richly rewarded by King Arthur, who makes him one of his Knights of the Round Table, and he lives happily ever after.

JACK THE GIANT KILLER

In this famous English folktale, Jack is the brave and inventive son of a Cornish farmer in the days of King Arthur. He fights and kills a whole series of giants. The first two are named Cormoran and Blunderbore. Jack then takes on a two-headed giant, whom he tricks into cutting his own stomach open.

King Arthur has now heard about Jack, and his son joins Jack on his adventures. When they meet a three-headed giant, they decide not to kill him, and in return the giant gives Jack a magic sword,

TROLL

A TROLL is a kind of giant, closely connected with stone. Trolls are very stupid but still highly dangerous. They have a close connection with rocks and are often found in caverns deep inside mountains.

BLOCK HEADS

Trolls are usually very big and greyish in color, with a large head and tiny eyes. In fact, they often look as if they are made from rock. Many Cave Trolls, who live in caverns deep within mountains, can only go outside at night and will actually turn to stone if sunlight touches them.

Most Trolls are extremely stupid and have poor eyesight, but they can still be very dangerous, since they weigh a lot and have enormous strength. If a Troll grabs hold of you, you're pretty much done for. Trolls are also very aggressive and will attack for no apparent reason.

Some Trolls are more intelligent and are good at building things. In Scandinavia, Trolls often build bridges and then live under them, like the Troll which tried to eat the Three Billy Goats Gruff in the famous fairy tale. This kind of Troll seems to be able to stand sunlight without turning to stone, but is just as mean and aggressive as the other kind. There are many stories of these Trolls deliberately attacking people who are happy and are having a good time.

Ogre

ORC

A kind of goblin, very strong and bred for fighting.

Orcs look like short, wide human beings, but they're immensely strong. They're cunning and treacherous. They can endure great hardship, ignore pain, and travel long distances on foot, in a sort of jogging run.

Orcs live only to fight. It's their purpose in life. They were originally bred by an evil magician to be a fighting force. They may do some stealing, bullying, and getting drunk in between fights. They only eat meat, and there have been rumors that they're not too fussy about eating each other.

Orcs were first mentioned in the famous books by J. R. R. Tolkien.

OGRE

A very ugly human-eating giant, often covered with hair.

Ogres are usually giants, though they may not be very big, as giants go. However, they make up for that by being extremely ugly—in fact, they are quite hideous to look at. But the main thing about an ogre that makes it truly unpleasant is that it eats people and is always hungry. Fortunately, ogres are not usually very clever so it is quite easy to outwit them if you are smart.

Orc

THE
CASTLE

GARGOYLE

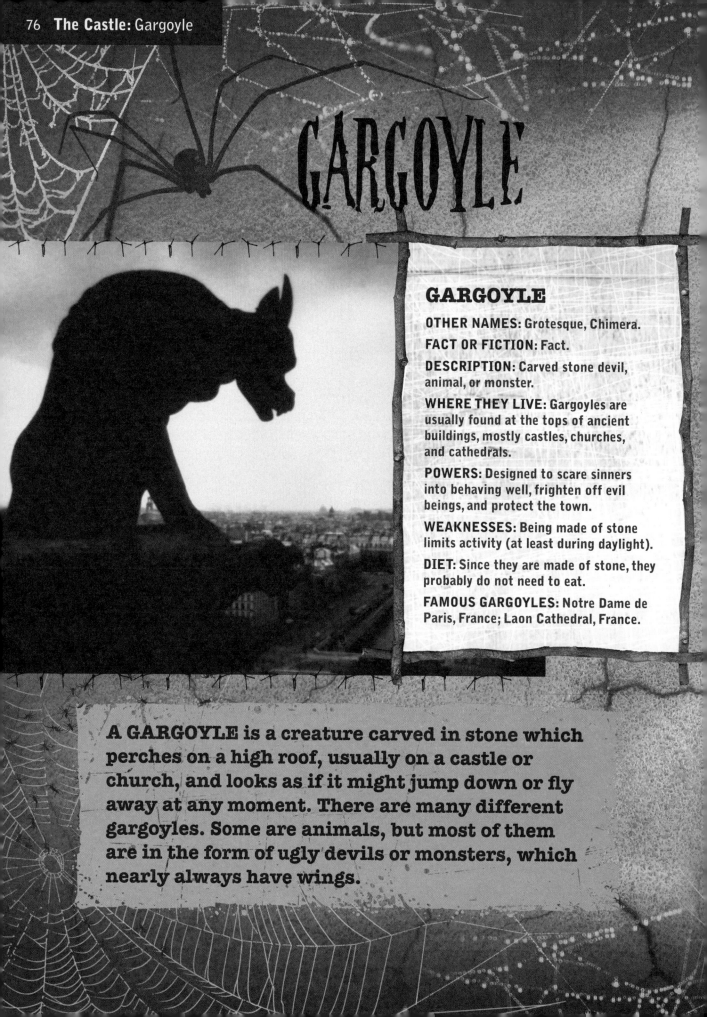

GARGOYLE

OTHER NAMES: Grotesque, Chimera.

FACT OR FICTION: Fact.

DESCRIPTION: Carved stone devil, animal, or monster.

WHERE THEY LIVE: Gargoyles are usually found at the tops of ancient buildings, mostly castles, churches, and cathedrals.

POWERS: Designed to scare sinners into behaving well, frighten off evil beings, and protect the town.

WEAKNESSES: Being made of stone limits activity (at least during daylight).

DIET: Since they are made of stone, they probably do not need to eat.

FAMOUS GARGOYLES: Notre Dame de Paris, France; Laon Cathedral, France.

A GARGOYLE is a creature carved in stone which perches on a high roof, usually on a castle or church, and looks as if it might jump down or fly away at any moment. There are many different gargoyles. Some are animals, but most of them are in the form of ugly devils or monsters, which nearly always have wings.

WATERSPOUTS BUT WHY SO SCARY?

The official explanation for gargoyles is that they were originally put on roofs to act as waterspouts. The word "gargoyle" is connected to "gurgle" and "gargle." The rainwater would run down the roof of the building into gutters and then through the gargoyles, which would act like fountains to project the water outward through their mouths and prevent it from soaking into the stone walls and damaging the building. But that doesn't explain why the gargoyles were made in the form of devils and monsters, or why many gargoyles actually aren't water-spouts at all, but just statues.

Many gargoyles are on churches and cathedrals, so the big mystery is: Why are such evil-looking creatures up there on the roof of a holy building? One theory is that they're intended to frighten people as they go in and out of the church to worship— showing them what evil things are waiting to punish them if they leave the protection of the church.

GUARD DEVILS

Another idea is that they're tame devils, and are there to protect the building. In the same way as a guard-dog would protect you against wolves, the gargoyles are there to guard the building against bigger and nastier devils who might come by. The fact that nobody's seen any of the bigger and nastier devils simply means the gargoyles are doing a good job. This would explain why they often seem to be watching out across the rooftops, rather than looking down at the people below. They're on the look-out for anything really bad that might fly past.

PROTECTING THE TOWN

In medieval times, the church was at the center of a town's society, and its gargoyles were seen to be protecting the whole town. Although they're trapped in stone during the day, some were believed to fly free at night and patrol the skies over the town, keeping everybody safe from any passing demons, unfriendly dragons, or other evil beings.

Although gargoyles are ugly and scary to look at, they're unlikely to harm you; although if you stand in the wrong place, they might spout water down onto your head. Some experts advise that gargoyles dislike being photographed, so it's better only to take photos of them when they're looking the other way.

Opposite and right: Gargoyles from Notre Dame Cathedral in Paris.

VAMPIRE

VAMPIRE

OTHER NAMES: Bloodsucker, Nosferatu.

FACT OR FICTION: Fiction.

DESCRIPTION: Pale, often almost transparent skin. Staring, sometimes bloodshot eyes. Blood-red lips; long, sharp canine teeth (which they try to hide from victims until they need them). Some have very long fingernails, like claws. Some vampires wear cloaks.

WHERE THEY LIVE: Many parts of the world, especially Eastern Europe. They are usually found in graves or coffins by day.

POWERS: Strong, fast, can hypnotize people and change into bats, wolves, or even mist.

WEAKNESSES: Repelled by garlic, salt, crucifixes, bright sunlight, running water, holy water, and silver blades. They can be killed by decapitation or by a stake through the heart.

DIET: Blood, blood, and more blood.

OTHER CHARACTERISTICS: A vampire casts no shadow and can't be seen reflected in a mirror.

FAMOUS VAMPIRES: Serbian peasants Arnold Paole and Peter Plogojowitz, Count Dracula.

VAMPIRES are dead people who have come back to life and feed on the blood of the living. They obtain it by biting people's necks and drinking their blood. If you are bitten by a vampire, unfortunately you will not only die but also become one too. Thankfully, there are several steps you can take to protect yourself.

Above left: The Empusa was a female vampire from Greek mythology that feasted on the blood of men.

ON THE HUNT

Venturing out at night, a vampire can take on the form of a bat or a wolf, or even drift around as a cloud of vapor. Confronting its prey, it hypnotizes the person, bites into their veins, and draws blood until satisfied. The victim feels no pain and later remembers little of the encounter—the only sign may be two puncture marks on the neck made by the vampire's teeth. Gradually, however, the victim will feel woozy and weak and will eventually pass away—only to awake from death as a vampire!

NIGHT LOVERS

Vampires are usually the corpses of criminals, suicides, or heretics—people who rejected Christianity. They sleep by day, but at night they rise up and venture forth to quench their thirst for blood.

Most often their daytime resting place is the grave where they were buried. But they can survive in their coffins elsewhere, as long as the coffin contains some soil from their original burial ground. Vampires have also been known to rest in cupboards rather than coffins, hanging upside down like bats. Castles are favored hideouts for vampires, since they are often far away from other houses, good for keeping nosy people out, and full of dark, spooky rooms.

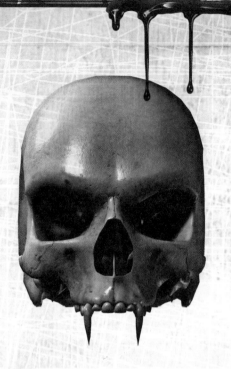

PUBLICITY AND PANIC

From the seventeenth century onward, belief in vampires was especially strong in the Austro-Hungarian Empire of eastern Europe. Dozens of cases were reported in the early 1700s, including two in rural Serbia—Arnold Paole, who was said to have murdered 16 people after he died, and Peter Plogojowitz, whose resurrected corpse supposedly snacked on and killed several of his neighbors. In both cases (and others), Austrian authorities dug up the body, proclaimed it a true vampire, drove a stake through the heart, and then issued a public report, which of course created widespread panic across Europe for many years.

BLOODSUCKERS ABOUND

Stories of spirits who feast on the blood of the living have been told around the world for thousands of years. Blood-drinking demons were reported in ancient India, Persia, and Assyria. In Greek mythology, the Empusa is a female monster that sucks the blood out of young men. In Roman myths the Strix is an owl-like bird that bites humans to obtain blood (see page 158).

Chinese folklore tells of the Jiang Shi (meaning "stiff corpse"), which hops around on its rigid legs with its arms outstretched and grabs and kills humans to suck out their life essence, or qi. The Penanggalan of Malaysia is a demonic woman whose fanged head separates from her body at night and flies around sucking blood from victims.

Right: Hungarian countess, Elizabeth Báthory.

OUT OF TRANSYLVANIA

Two unpleasant historical figures became associated with vampire legends, even though there was little evidence that they had ever bitten anyone in the neck. Vlad Tepes or Vlad the Impaler, ruler of Transylvania in Romania from 1431 to 1476, was also known as Dracula, meaning "son of the dragon." He was renowned for his bloodlust and often killed his enemies by impaling them on sharpened stakes. Hungarian countess Elizabeth Báthory kidnapped and murdered young peasants and bathed in their blood, believing this would preserve her youth.

These two stories and other eastern European legends had a powerful influence on nineteenth-century writers, most notably Irish author Bram Stoker, who in 1897 published the novel, *Dracula*. This in turn became the source of many of our modern ideas about vampires, and the inspiration for numerous books and films.

Above: Vlad the Impaler and his castle.

DRACULA

In Bram Stoker's novel, *Dracula*, Count Dracula lives in a crumbling castle in Transylvania. A visiting Englishman, Jonathan Harker, discovers that the count is a vampire. Managing to escape from the castle, Harker flees to England, but Dracula has his followers transport him there in a coffin and turns one of Harker's friends, Lucy, into a vampire. Soon after, Dracula starts attacking Harker's fiancée, Mina. Dracula runs back to Romania, but Harker follows him and kills him, which is the only way that Mina can be saved.

KEEPING VAMPIRES AT BAY

You're safe from vampires by day, since they will always shun daylight. Sprinkling salt or holy water along your doorstep and windowsills and hanging a bunch of garlic on the door will prevent a vampire from entering your house after dark.

If you have to go out at night, carry garlic with you or, even better, a crucifix— hold it up to a vampire and it will back off quickly. Jumping into or across a river is another way to escape, since vampires loathe running water.

ALL AT STAKE

Getting rid of a vampire for good is tricky, but there are at least a few options. One is to destroy its hiding place and trap it outdoors —it will gradually die if exposed to sunlight, though this could take some time. Another, quicker option is to decapitate it with a grave-digger's spade. But the most popular and proven method is to hammer a sharpened wooden stake—preferably from an elder tree—through the vampire's heart. To make sure the vampire never rises again, you have to burn the corpse or bury it in a new grave, ideally near a crossroads.

MINOTAUR

THE MINOTAUR is a savage creature of Greek mythology, half-man, half-bull. Kept by King Minos of Crete in his palace complex at Knossos, he was fed live humans for many years, until he was killed by the hero Theseus.

IN THE LABYRINTH

The Minotaur was the monstrous offspring of Minos's wife, Pasiphae, and a white bull sent to Minos by the god Poseidon. To restrain the beast, Minos had it placed at the center of an almost impenetrable labyrinth, or maze. When Minos's son, Androgeos, was killed in Athens, Minos demanded compensation. So, every nine years, the Athenians sent him seven young men and seven young women, and Minos would drive them into the labyrinth to be devoured by the Minotaur.

THESEUS THE HERO

Appalled by the monster, the Athenian warrior Theseus decided he would kill the monster and volunteered to be sent to Knossos as one of the seven young men. When he arrived, Minos's daughter, Ariadne, fell in love with him. Before he entered the labyrinth, she gave him a ball of thread and a sword. Theseus unraveled the thread as he traveled to the center of the labyrinth and, after killing the Minotaur, followed it back to the entrance and escaped from Crete with Ariadne.

FRANKENSTEIN'S MONSTER

Mary Shelley's 1818 novel, *Frankenstein*, describes the creation of one of the most famous storybook monsters.

Swiss scientist Victor Frankenstein decides to make a human-like creature out of body parts he steals from graveyards. But the creature is so hideous—8 ft (2.5 m) tall with a huge head and ugly yellow skin—that he abandons it. After the monster kills his brother, Frankenstein flees to England, then Ireland, but the monster follows him and murders his bride. Desperate to escape, Frankenstein sails to the Arctic, but is pursued by his creation, and both die amid the ice.

RED CAP

If you visit a ruined castle along the border between England and Scotland, watch out for these fearsome goblins.

Red Caps are said to murder travelers and use their blood to dye their hats red, and they must do this often because they die if their hats dry out or fade. Don't try to flee if you see one, however. For although they look like tiny old men and are weighed down by iron boots, they can run like the wind and have long, talon-like claws to grip and rip. Much better to stand your ground and hold up a crucifix or recite words from the Bible. That sends them scurrying for cover.

WIZARD

OTHER NAMES: Magician, sorcerer, warlock, enchanter, magus, alchemist, shaman.

FACT OR FICTION: Fiction, though many people throughout history have claimed to be wizards.

DESCRIPTION: Usually, wizards are men with long white hair and beards. They wear robes, a cape (often covered with stars or magical symbols) and a pointed hat, and carry a staff or magic wand.

WHERE THEY LIVE: Richer wizards inhabit castles and towers, though some of these may be old ruins. Others live in caves and forest hollows.

POWERS: Wizards can create magic potions, cast spells, hypnotize people, see into and influence the future, and change themselves and other people into animals.

WEAKNESSES: Often old, so they tend to be a little slow moving. But don't let appearances deceive—their magic works fast and is powerful!

OTHER CHARACTERISTICS: Interested in the magical properties of numbers and astrology.

FAMOUS WIZARDS: Merlin, Dr. John Dee, Nicolas Flamel, Nostradamus, Gandalf, Dumbledore, Harry Potter.

WIZARDS, who are usually men, use magic and spells to make things happen. Many are good and employ their powers to help others, but some, especially those known as sorcerers, prefer to taunt, terrify, and torment. Good magic is known as "white magic," whereas magic used for evil purposes is "black magic."

CASTING A SPELL

Wizards call up supernatural spirits and forces and make them work on their behalf. They do this by casting spells. Casting a spell might involve chanting a series of phrases while making certain gestures, or giving someone a potion to drink.

Before performing a spell, a wizard may draw a circle on the ground with chalk or salt, known as a magic circle. He may place the items required for the spell inside this circle to concentrate its power, or he may stand inside it when pronouncing the spell, to protect himself from the dangerous forces he is unleashing.

CONTROLLING NATURE

Wizards have power over the elements—air, earth, fire, and water. So they can provoke storms, floods, fires, and even earthquakes.

Some can call upon evil demons to do their dirty work, including mandragoras, tiny servants of the devil. Others can turn into other creatures at will—and even fly.

WIZARD WAYS

In some societies wizards are important figures. But in others they are outcasts, often feared and despised, who live alone in remote towers and have to be sought out by people who need their help. Wizards learn their magic from older wizards. They compile libraries of books of spells, and store jars full of magical plants and other substances for making potions. Every wizard needs a staff or wand to channel and direct his magic. It is usually made of wood and sometimes decorated with magical symbols. Without it, spells may be less effective or not work at all.

ANIMAL COMPANIONS

Like witches, wizards also have companions, known as familiars. These are supernatural spirits that assume the form of animals—most often cats, toads, owls, and rats— to help and protect the wizard.

Below: Merlin and King Arthur find the sword, Excalibur.

MERLIN

Apart from Harry Potter, probably the most famous wizard of all is Merlin, who appears in the old English legends of King Arthur. The character was based on a sixth-century Welsh hermit called Myrddin. In some of the legends, Merlin is a sinister sorcerer, renowned for his shape-shifting. However, in others he is King Arthur's kindly adviser and protector. When he was very old, Merlin decided to share his wizard secrets with the woman Niviane, whom he loved. However, she was deceitful and used Merlin's powers against him to trap him in a tomb forever.

SECOND SIGHT

Any decent wizard should be able to predict the future—a practice known as divination or scrying. To do this, he might rely on second sight, which are visions simply popping into his head, or he might peer into a crystal ball (a common wizard tool) and see future events unfolding there.

The early sixteenth-century French wizard Michel de Nostradame, also known as Nostradamus, had his own particular technique. He would fill a bowl with water and place it on a brass tripod. After touching his wand to the tripod, the water and his robe, he would stare into the water, waiting for images of the future to appear. Eventually, he wrote them all down as verses. After some appeared to come true, he was invited to work at the court of the king, Henri II of France.

THE PHILOSOPHER'S STONE

In the Middle Ages, many wizards became obsessed with discovering a method for turning common metals into gold, a practice known as alchemy. In turn, they thought this would give them the power to cure all illness and let people live forever. The key to making all this happen was thought to be a substance called the Philosopher's Stone. Searching for the stone, wizards pored over ancient books, ground up minerals, boiled chemicals, and whipped up potions.

Frenchman Nicolas Flamel claimed to have found the Philosopher's Stone in the early 1400s. No evidence to support his claim has been found—though he did die a very wealthy man.

THE GRAVEYARD

ZOMBIE

ZOMBIE

OTHER NAMES: Zonbi, nzumbe.

FACT OR FICTION: There are many stories of their existence. No genuine Zombies have ever been scientifically examined, though there are scientific theories about how "zombification" might actually happen.

DESCRIPTION: May look almost like a normal person or may be in a state of decay. Has a typically glazed or "hypnotized"'stare. Moves slowly. Seldom speaks. Cannot feel pain.

WHERE THEY LIVE: Most common in Haiti, but also known to occur in other Caribbean islands and in West Africa and South Africa.

POWERS: Zombies do not possess any special magic powers, but they can terrify living people just by their appearance.

WEAKNESSES: Have no mind or will-power of their own and can act only in obedience to commands.

DIET: Zombies like to eat humans, especially brains. However, if a Zombie can be made to eat salt, that will make it return to its grave.

OTHER CHARACTERISTICS: Very popular in horror films and comics.

A ZOMBIE is a dead person that has been brought back to life. Through the use of magic, the Zombie can be made to walk around and do things, but it is not truly alive and is usually under the control of a magician. The idea of Zombies originated in the Voodoo religions of Africa and the Caribbean.

THE BOKOR

Most of the stories of Zombies in films and books have originated from Haitian legends. There is still a widespread belief in Haiti that Zombies are possible and have existed.

A Zombie can only be created by a "bokor," a Voodoo magician who practices "magic of the left hand" or black magic. It is believed that, through the use of spells and drugs, the bokor captures a person's soul. The person quickly falls ill and dies. After they have been buried, the bokor raises the corpse from the dead and makes it his slave. As long as he keeps its soul, the Zombie has lost its personality and free will and can only act to carry out the bokor's commands. However, it is a dangerous creature since it feels no pain and cannot be killed, and the fear that it inspires makes sure that the bokor will get whatever he wants from the living.

Usually, the Zombie walks slowly and has a fixed stare. It may decay in the same way as a corpse in the grave, but it will keep walking and obeying the bokor's orders until it really falls apart, at which point the sorcerer may have to get a new one.

ZOMBIES IN AFRICA

The Zombie legends really originate in Africa, where the Voodoo religion came from.

West Africa In West African tradition, the part of the soul that the bokor captures is called the Zombie Astral. It is believed that sorcerers keep a number of these spirits in glass jars and can use them for magical purposes. On payment of a fee, you can buy the influence of a Zombie Astral for good or evil purposes, though they lose their strength after a time.

South Africa In South African legends, Zombies may be dead or can be living people who have been taken over by a sorcerer and are kept in a trance-like state. They can be created by witches and even by children who are unaware of their own magic powers and can call up the dead without knowing it. A powerful witch doctor can break the spell.

There's a legend of the Zombie Train, which looks from a distance like a train full of people but is actually full of Zombies under the control of a witch. Unsuspecting living people who board the train at night are either flung off again into the desert, or are forced to join the Zombies as a slave laborer.

A SCIENTIFIC EXPLANATION FOR ZOMBIES?

In the 1980s, a Canadian scientist, Wade Davis, studied several cases of apparent real-life Zombies. He concluded that these people had never actually died, but had been drugged into a deep coma, declared dead, and buried. The bokor had then dug them up and revived them by administering further powerful drugs. From then on, they were kept in a permanently drugged state by the bokor; they also believed that they had died and were Zombies and so accepted their new life. The drugs included the powerful poison tetrodotoxin, extracted from the puffer fish, and the plant extract datura. Some of Davis's work has been questioned by other scientists, but it seems likely that the use of drugs, as well as forms of mental illness, would explain many of the Zombie legends.

MOVIE ZOMBIES

In most horror films about Zombies, there is no controlling sorcerer and the Zombies are an independent race of the undead with an overwhelming desire to eat living people, particularly the brains which are their favorite delicacy. People who are bitten by Zombies become Zombies themselves. This makes for more exciting stories, but is invented and not part of the original legend.

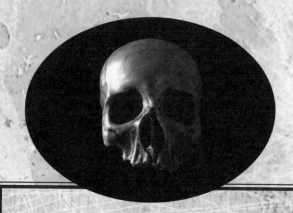

GHOUL

A creature that lives in graveyards and eats corpses.

It's not clear whether Ghouls start out as people or then become transformed into undead monsters through eating human flesh, or whether they are spirit beings to begin with. They are only seen at night so it's possible that daylight, and also fire, may harm them. They look a little human, but are very pale, tall, and thin with long claw-like hands. They seem to haunt the same graveyards for centuries, so they are probably immortal. They like to travel in groups and seem to enjoy their grave-robbing work, since their hideous laughter can be heard from a distance. Humans who enjoy the misery of others are sometimes described as "ghoulish."

DOKKAEBI

Korean spirits, which can be kind or otherwise, depending on how you behave.

A Dokkaebi in its natural state is roughly human-shaped with a red face, bulging eyes, and one or two horns on its head. It is covered in fur and carries a stick or club, which is really a magic wand. The chances of seeing a Dokkaebi looking like this are slim, because it has the ability to transform itself into anything at any time and has a hat that can make it invisible. It can also transform objects into other things using its club or wand.

These spirits are unpredictable and easily annoyed, but they're kind to good-hearted people. They tend to go out looking for trouble and will torment anyone they decide to pick on, though usually with good reason. They're ignorant and rough, and rather too fond of a drink, but like to give themselves airs and show off their magic powers.

Many Korean folktales tell of face-to-face encounters with Dokkaebi and even of people who became good friends with one. Mostly, they jump out on you in quiet places like graveyards and try to frighten or bully you, but it's possible to outsmart them.

Below: A Necromancer invokes a spirit.

information from the dead and therefore become more powerful himself.

The rituals of Necromancy are complicated and require a high level of magic knowledge. Parts of dead bodies are believed to be used in the rituals and so Necromancers often deal with Ghouls and other graveyard inhabitants.

GRAVE ROBBER

Someone who digs up graves and removes the contents in order to sell them.

Many people in past cultures were buried with their valuable belongings, for example the ancient Egyptians, the Aztecs and Mayans of South America, and the Native Americans of North America. Throughout history, criminals have been known to dig up these graves and steal the precious artifacts to sell. Many believe that such treasure is cursed and that even archaeologists who take it to show in museums will suffer as a result.

NECROMANCER

A magician who specializes in summoning the spirits of the dead.

A Necromancer practices black magic, or more specifically, anything associated with death and usually involving rituals to summon and question the spirits of the dead. Necromancy is considered to be a particularly dangerous form of black magic, because it attempts to break down the barrier between the living and the dead— usually so that the Necromancer can gain

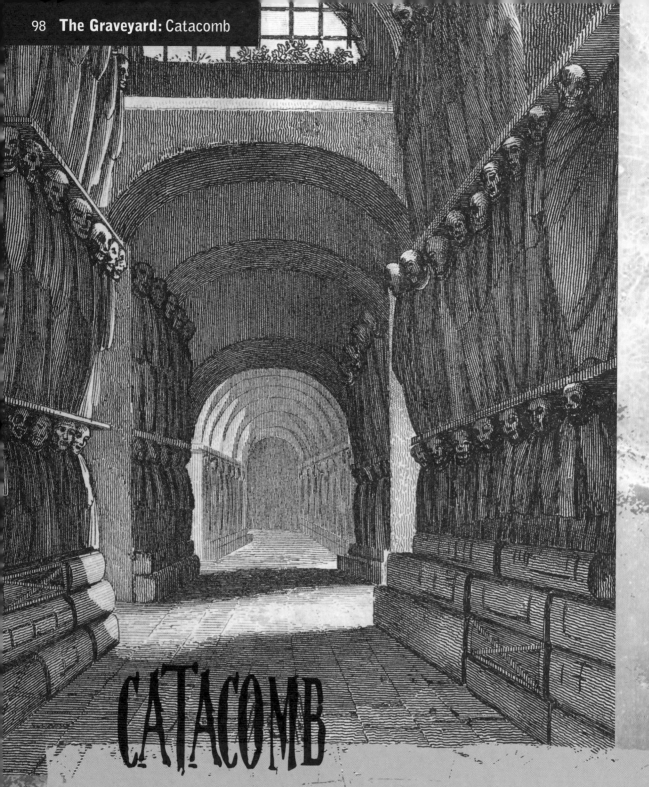

CATACOMB

A CATACOMB is an underground burial chamber, usually very large and containing the remains of many dead people. Most catacombs, however, have been unused for a very long time. They have been used as meeting places for all kinds of people who want to keep out of the public eye—from smugglers to people interested in witchcraft.

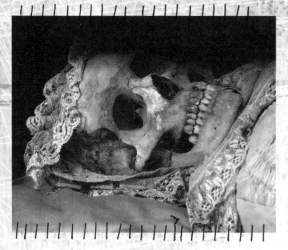

ROME CATACOMBS

The best-known and oldest catacombs are in Rome, Italy, where many people, including some of the earliest Popes, were buried. Other European cities later built catacombs and in a few places they continued to be used until the twentieth century, although in most countries it became more usual to bury the dead in cemeteries or in crypts under churches.

PARIS CATACOMBS

The catacombs that lie under the city of Paris, France, are an ossuary, or place where the skeletal remains of people are kept. Since the time of the ancient Romans, the remains of about six million people have been collected here.

THE SLEEPING DEAD

The process of decay is slower in a catacomb than for a burial in a grave, and coffins remain intact in catacombs for a very long time. There are a few catacombs, such as the one in Palermo, Sicily in Italy, where the bodies have been embalmed and are not in coffins but on display in alcoves and on shelves, some sitting in chairs. There are about 8,000 dead here, some still very well preserved but others now reduced to skeletons.

Below: The catacombs in Rome, Italy.

Opposite: The catacombs in Palermo, Sicily in Italy.

SCREAMING SKULL

The skull of a murder victim that cries out for vengeance.

There are many legends of screaming skulls. Usually, the skull belonged to someone who was murdered, but the murderer was never brought to justice. In some stories, the skull is accidentally dug up, and takes the opportunity to give the finder a scare by screaming at them and then demanding their help in getting revenge. There is a famous story of a screaming skull from Dorset in England, which is the skull of an African slave who asked to be buried in his native land, but whose wishes were not respected.

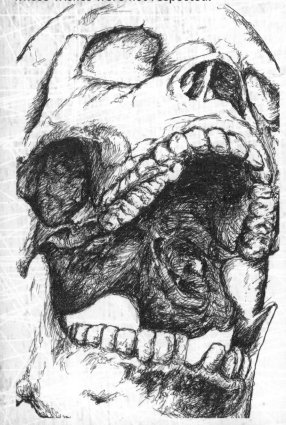

SKELETON WARRIOR

An undead skeletal fighter with an evil nature.

A Skeleton Warrior is similar to a Zombie, since it is raised from the dead by a powerful magician, who then controls it completely. However, as its name suggests, a Skeleton Warrior is an animated set of bones with all the flesh removed. These Warriors usually wear some form of armor to help keep their bones together, but, being undead, they are more or less indestructible.

Skeleton Warriors generally have very nasty natures, because the magic used to create them will only work on someone who, in life, was particularly evil-hearted.

It's really a bad idea to get into a fight with a Skeleton Warrior, unless you're a powerful magician yourself.

HEADLESS HORSEMAN

A headless ghost rider on a horse who brings a sense of impending doom.

Headless Horsemen appear all over the world in legends. They are very frightening and to see one is generally a sign that something bad is going to happen. Headless Horsemen often ride a grey horse and wear a long grey coat. Sometimes they carry their head tucked under their arm or propped on the saddle in front of them. In German legend, the Headless Horseman seeks out those who have gone unpunished for crimes.

In the folklore of Cornwall, England, a Horseman with half a face and half a head roams the moors looking for souls to steal.

There are many Headless Horseman stories in the United States. Most date back to the Civil War, but the most famous one appears in the story *The Legend of Sleepy Hollow* by Washington Irving (published 1820). This Horseman is supposedly a soldier whose head has been blown off by a cannonball during the American Revolution. Despite being buried in the graveyard of the peaceful small town of Sleepy Hollow, the Horseman cannot rest, but wanders at night, attacking the living. He even uses his head as a weapon, hurling it with tremendous force to strike down his victim.

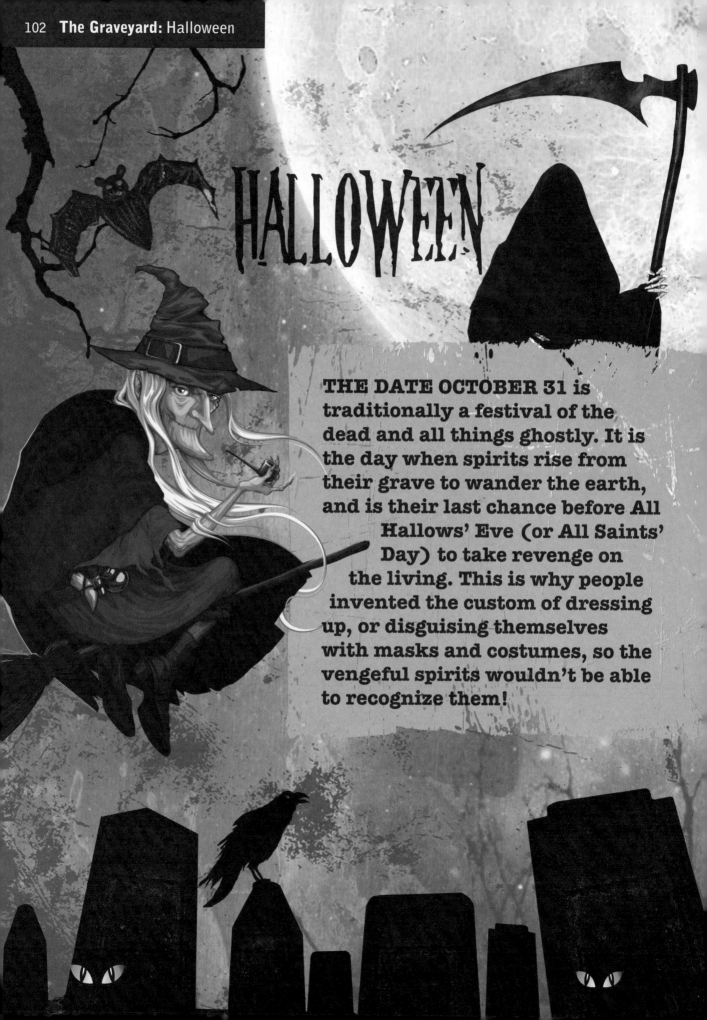

HALLOWEEN

THE DATE OCTOBER 31 is traditionally a festival of the dead and all things ghostly. It is the day when spirits rise from their grave to wander the earth, and is their last chance before All Hallows' Eve (or All Saints' Day) to take revenge on the living. This is why people invented the custom of dressing up, or disguising themselves with masks and costumes, so the vengeful spirits wouldn't be able to recognize them!

ALL HALLOWS' EVE

The word Halloween was originally All Hallows' Eve, meaning the day before All Hallows or All Saints' Day, which is on November 1. All Saints' is a particularly holy day for many Christians and is followed by All Souls' Day on November 2, when prayers are said for the dead and families visit the graves of their loved ones. So, in many parts of the world, this is a season when the lands of the dead and the living are less separated than usual, when the dead are remembered and respected and may come to visit their families and friends. In many countries, Halloween is considered to be the day when evil spirits are abroad, before the two holy days that renew the influence of good in the world.

Since Halloween is the last chance for restless spirits to wander the earth and take vengeance on the living, Halloween is definitely the night when anything evil—from demons to witches—will come out to play.

AUTUMN FESTIVAL

In northern countries, Halloween is very much an autumn festival and includes traditions to do with the food of the season, like apples (bobbing) and pumpkins (jack o'lanterns). In modern times, it has also become associated with dressing-up in costume as witches, wizards, and monsters of various kinds, holding parties, and "trick-or-treating," but this harmless fun should not make us forget the deeply spooky nature of Halloween.

ANCIENT ORIGINS

The ancient Celtic festival of Samhain was at about the same time as Halloween. It marked the end of the "lighter half" of the year and the beginning of the "darker half" and was also a festival of the harvest. It is believed that Samhain was the start of the New Year for ancient Celtic societies. Some of the Samhain rituals have been developed over the centuries into more modern festivities. For instance, bonfires were very important at Samhain, and these are now part of Halloween in many countries, while in England they're part of Guy Fawkes' or Firework Night (November 5). Masks and costumes were worn at Samhain to keep evil spirits away, and candles were lit and placed inside large hollowed-out turnips with faces carved on them—both of these traditions have survived into the modern Halloween, though now we use pumpkins to make the jack o'lantern with its toothy grin. Importantly, Samhain was believed to be the time when the dead could access the living world and when extra care must be taken to honor them and make them welcome if they chose to visit. Places might be set for the dead at a family's Samhain feast.

DRESSING UP

The ancient idea behind Halloween costumes was that, if you were masked and disguised, the evil spirits or unhappy ghosts wouldn't know who you were and couldn't harm you. If you dressed as a witch or ghost, they might even think you were one of their own kind. Most people have forgotten this original idea and now see Halloween as a chance to dress up as a character from a horror film or from a well-known series of books about wizards.

TRICK OR TREAT

This part of Halloween has long been popular in the USA and in recent years has been adopted in the UK and other countries too. Groups of children in Halloween costumes will go around their neighborhood knocking on doors and asking for a "treat," which will usually be sweets. If the neighbor refuses, the children will play a mildly nasty "trick" such as throwing eggs at the house, or something similar. "Trick or treat" seems to be a combination of two ancient traditions —the Scottish custom of guising, where children and young people wore costumes for Halloween, and the Northern English Mischief Night, which was usually in early November, when practical jokes of all kinds were played, especially by children.

HALLOWEEN SUPERSTITIONS

- Never start a journey after sunset on Halloween.
- If you must go out on Halloween, carry bread and salt in your pocket.
- If you see a spider on Halloween, it may be the ghost of someone you used to know who is watching you.
- Girls wishing to know whom they will marry should sit in front of a mirror holding a candle, either combing their hair or eating an apple. They will see their future husband looking over their shoulder.
- If you put your clothes on inside out and walk backwards on Halloween, you will meet a witch.
- Carry a candle from 11pm until midnight. If the flame burns steadily you will be safe for the season, but if the spirits blow the flame out, you must beware of evil influences throughout the winter.

LAST CHANCE FOR REVENGE

One early Christian belief was that the souls of those who had died during the year wandered the earth until All Souls' Day, when they could finally rest. Any who felt they had been badly treated in life would be running out of time to get revenge, and would be especially dangerous in the last few days including Halloween.

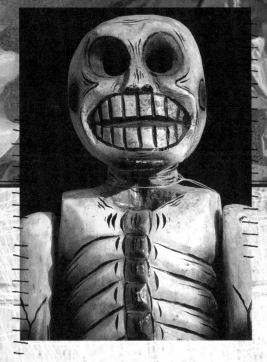

DAY OF THE DEAD

For centuries in Mexico, they have celebrated the Day of the Dead, or (in Spanish) Dia de los Muertos. This festival was to remember people's dead ancestors, and originally took place in August. However, after the arrival of the Spanish, who were Catholics, the festival was moved to coincide with All Saints' Day on November 1.

During the festival, people build altars in their houses in memory of their dead, and decorate the grave sites of their families with all sorts of things, from flowers and candles to food, photographs, and even toys (if the ancestor died as a child). The idea is that the dead might be coaxed into returning to the family for a reunion.

Skulls, skeletons, and even masks, cakes, and lollipops shaped like skulls are seen everywhere in Mexico on this day.

THE UNDER-WORLD

DEMON

DEMON

OTHER NAMES: Devil, Fallen Angel, fiend, Incubus, Succubus, evil spirit.

FACT OR FICTION: Many people believe demons to be fact.

DESCRIPTION: Like the Devil, demons are often shown with horns, wings, a tail and holding a forked trident, which looks a bit like a pitchfork. However, demons may take many forms and cultures around the world all have their own kinds of demons. Some demons may look like a normal human, but they may have hidden wings or a special mark on their body that shows they are not human but an evil demon. Demons can also take the form of beautiful women.

WHERE THEY LIVE: Demons can live anywhere, but obviously many prefer the dark and gloomy Underworld.

POWERS: Demons can be strong and fast, and many can also fly. Some are immune to flames or heat. They can play tricks on people's minds.

WEAKNESSES: Although demons cannot be killed, they can be banished if you know the right words to say.

DEMONS are evil spirits that are well known for tempting humans into behaving badly. Many people think that demons are a kind of angel that has gone bad, and they are often called "Fallen Angels." Like angels, demons may have wings, and many live in the Underworld and are immune to heat and fire.

FALLEN ANGELS

The original Greek word "daemon" means any kind of spirit, good or bad. The spelling "demon" is generally used to describe the very powerful evil beings that are believed by many religions to exist and to be at work on earth. Demons are based in the Underworld, away from the light of goodness, but can move amongst us and are always looking for ways to get more power over human beings and the world we live in.

Demons are the equals of angels, and many of them are thought to be angels who have "fallen," or become bad. They're mostly invisible to humans, but when they do appear they often have a fiery appearance, as well as being connected with darkness.

Demons are associated with temptation and with people's dangerous weaknesses.

Traditionally, demons like a challenge, so there are many stories of a saint or a holy person being picked out by a demon as a good target for temptation and having to battle to keep control of their soul.

SEVEN DEADLY DEMONS

People from different religions have attempted to classify and describe demons. One of the most famous Christian classifications lists the demons who are linked to the Seven Deadly Sins and who will try to tempt you to indulge:

Lucifer Demon of pride (though Lucifer is also used as a name for the Devil).

Mammon Demon of money and the love of money.

Asmodeus Demon of lust and passion.

Leviathan Demon of envy.

Beelzebub Demon of gluttony and greed.

Amon Demon of rage.

Belphegor Demon of sloth and idleness.

These demons, sometimes called the Princes of Hell, all have other evil work to do, but these particular sins are their areas of special interest.

CERBERUS

CERBERUS was a huge and terrifying dog who sat at the gates of the Underworld from ancient Greek mythology. He had three heads and was sometimes shown with a mane of live snakes and a snake tail.

ORPHEUS RESCUES EURYDICE

Orpheus, the legendary musician, was one of the few living people to get past Cerberus. He needed to get into the Underworld to rescue his beloved wife Eurydice. He lulled Cerberus to sleep with beautiful music, and was able to plead with Hades, the god of the Underworld, to release Eurydice. Hades agreed, but only on the condition that Orpheus let Eurydice follow him and didn't look back at her until both were above ground. The two of them passed the still-sleeping Cerberus and were almost above ground when Orpheus looked back, and lost Eurydice forever.

GUARD DOG

Cerberus's task was to stop living people from entering the Underworld and to stop anyone at all from getting out. He was once kidnapped by Hercules who captured him as one of the "labors" or tasks that he had to fulfill to appease King Eurythseus. But Cerberus was so hideous that when Hercules triumphantly brought the dog to Eurythseus, he was told to take him straight back to the Underworld again.

HEL AND GARM

HEL is the goddess who rules Helheim. She decides how the dead are going to live through eternity in her realm. Garm is Hel's dog, who guards the entrance to the Underworld.

THE GATES OF HELHEIM

Helheim is the Underworld in Norse mythology. It's gloomy and contains many vast houses with very high walls. Not all the dead go there, only those who die of sickness or old age. Those who die bravely, for example in battle, go to Valhalla which is a much more cheerful place. Helheim is not the same as Hell. Hell is extremely hot and all the souls who go there are tortured, while in Helheim they mostly just lead a very sad and quiet life.

The ruler of Helheim, the goddess Hel, is tall, thin, dark, bony, and fierce. She can be merciless—when the god Baldr died and the other gods begged her to let him come back to the living, she said she would only do so if everyone on earth wept for him. One giant refused to weep and so Hel kept Baldr with her for eternity.

Hel's dog, Garm, looks like a huge hunting dog, but has four eyes and is always dripping with blood. It is said that the darkness of Helheim hangs around him.

HELLHOUND

A hound that comes and goes between the Underworld and the living world.

Unlike the guardians of the Underworld such as Cerberus and Garm, Hellhounds live in the Underworld but are free to roam in the world above, as big black dogs with red eyes who inspire terror in all human beings who see them.

Known all over the world, they may hunt in a pack, but they're most often seen alone in desolate places. Stories of Hellhounds are very ancient in Britain. One hound, called the Black Shuck, has been seen in the counties of Essex, Norfolk, and Suffolk since before even the Vikings came. Each time he appears, at least one person who sees him dies soon after. He once ran through a church, leaving scorch marks behind him, and two people who were praying dropped dead on the spot.

Left: Hellhound.
Above right: Fomorii.

FOMORII

Ancient Irish tribe, thought to come up from the Underworld.

The Fomorii or Fomorians lived on an island off the coast of Donegal and frequently attacked other tribes of ancient Ireland. They were violent and ugly—sometimes described as having goats' heads or having one foot, one arm, and one eye each—and were known to have access to Hell.

FURY

THE FURIES were terrifying and hideous goddesses of justice and revenge. Three sisters, they all had leathery wings, snakes for hair, and blood dripping from their eyes.

TOUGH BUT FAIR

The names of the three Furies, from ancient Greek mythology, were Megaera ("the jealous one"), Alecto ("unceasing anger") and Tisiphone ("avenger of murder"). They were also known as the Daughters of the Night. Sometimes they lived in the Underworld, but mostly they were among the living, hunting down evil-doers.

The Furies would punish any crime, but especially offenses against the gods and crimes within the family such as violence toward a family member. The crime they hated most was the murder of a parent. They never gave up and would pursue offenders to the ends of the earth if necessary. Their favorite punishment was to make criminals go mad—in fact, knowing that the Furies were after them was enough to make most people go insane anyway.

However, the Furies were completely fair—they always knew the truth about any crime and would never punish anyone who was innocent. They could also defend the weak, and would protect beggars and wanderers, and also some animals.

HARPY

FLESH EATERS

Harpies were always hungry for flesh of any kind, and would steal food, even from a king's table. The word "harpy" comes from a Greek word meaning "to grab" or "to snatch," and Harpies were most famous for seizing people and taking them away to the Underworld, where they would torture them and tear them to pieces.

Unlike the Furies, the Harpies were not fair judges: they might drag you off to the Underworld on instructions from one of the gods, you might have committed a crime and deserved punishment—or you might just be unlucky. You could be innocent and they'd take you anyway because they were hungry.

Some legends say they were a living form of the harsh winter winds, that cause destruction to anything that happens to be in their path. If people disappeared unexpectedly, it was thought that the Harpies might have taken them.

HARPIES were monsters from ancient Greek mythology. They were huge birds with the heads of (usually ugly) women, and big sharp claws. They were vicious and permanently hungry and could take you to the Underworld.

Dark Dwarf

The Dark Dwarves are ancient beings in mythology. They were formed from the maggots that ate the flesh of the great giant, Ymir, who was the first living thing to be created in the world, according to Norse legend. However, later they were given the gift of reason and became cunning. These Dwarves were clever craftsmen and made magical items for the gods, but they were considered untrustworthy and too fond of gold and treasure.

Oni

An Oni is a horned Japanese demon with big sharp teeth and appears in many legends. Onis often have red, green, or blue skin, and they always have horns, claws, and large, sharp, fang-like teeth. Oni dislike holly, which can be planted in your garden to keep them away from the house. It's best to keep them away, since they hunt for sinners to eat.

Ammut

Known as the Devourer of the Dead, Ammut was a monster, part hippopotamus and part lion with the head of a crocodile. She waited in the Underworld when the hearts of the dead were being weighed. If the dead person's heart was not pure enough to be allowed into Heaven, then the heart would be given to Ammut to eat, and the person's soul must wander forever.

Right: Ammut was a female demon from Egyptian mythology.

RIVER
AND
LAKE

LOCH NESS MONSTER

LOCH NESS MONSTER

OTHER NAMES: Nessie.

FACT OR FICTION: Scientists say fiction, but many people claim to have seen the monster and there are also photographs in existence (see opposite page).

DESCRIPTION: A huge serpentine creature with a long neck and a small head. It is about 30 ft (9 m) long in total and has at least one hump. It looks very much like a dinosaur, and many people believe that it might be a descendant of a dinosaur and has lived quietly in Loch Ness for millions of years.

WHERE THEY LIVE: Loch Ness—a large lake in Scotland.

POWERS: No magical powers, but due to its immense size, it's strong enough to overpower smaller creatures.

WEAKNESSES: It is obviously shy since it is rarely seen. It has only been seen in Loch Ness, so it clearly cannot travel further.

DIET: By all accounts the Loch Ness Monster is a carnivore, meaning that it eats meat—it has been seen with smaller creatures in its mouth.

THE LOCH NESS MONSTER is a creature that is said to live in the huge lake, called Loch Ness, in Scotland. Although scientists dismiss it as a hoax or a figment of the imagination, there are many supposed sightings of the creature both in the water and on land. Some think it is a dinosaur.

SIGHTINGS

Loch Ness is a large lake in Scotland—23 miles (37 km) wide and 755 ft (230 m) deep. Throughout history, there have been legends of a Loch Ness Monster, and since the twentieth century there have been many sightings and photographs of "Nessie."

Possibly the first report of the monster was by Saint Columba. He met the monster on land, near the Loch. It followed him but didn't dare attack because it recognized that he was a holy man.

That happened in the seventh century. Across the centuries that followed, there have been many stories about the beast. In 1933, a Mr. Spicer wrote to a London newspaper saying that he and his wife had been on vacation near Loch Ness and had seen a creature like "a dragon or a prehistoric animal," crossing the road in front of their car with a smaller animal in its mouth.

PHOTOGRAPHS

The first photographs of the monster date from the 1930s, showing it swimming with its head held above the water and with what seem to be humps on its back. Many other eyewitnesses have seen something similar, either in the Loch or walking clumsily near the shore. However, numerous scientific tests and expeditions have all failed to come up with any proof of Nessie's existence.

LAKE MONSTERS

Nessie is typical of the lake monsters that appear in local legends all over the world. Some 250 lakes have stories of similar beasts, and these lakes are quite similar—all are large and very deep, and the water in them is always cold; also, they all either connect with the sea or used to do so in earlier times.

No bodies or remains of the monsters have ever been found, and no live monsters have ever been caught. Nets and traps have been set, underwater cameras used, and teams of scientists have kept 24-hour watch for months without seeing anything. Yet people keep seeing strange creatures around these lakes.

MANIPOGO

A sociable monster that lives in Lake Manitoba.

The Manipogo, the monster that has been seen in Lake Manitoba (Canada) has been described as a huge brown snake with a long head like that of a horse or a sheep. Unusually, three Manipogos have been observed swimming around together—they were seen by a group of 17 eyewitnesses.

FLATHEAD LAKE MONSTER

A many-humped monster that lives in Flathead Lake.

The monster in Flathead Lake (Montana, USA) has been described as being like a giant eel, swimming in an undulating movement that gives the impression of a series of humps. It is blackish in color, very shiny, and has a round head. It was first reported in 1889 and has been seen regularly since, usually during the spring and summer months.

SILVER LAKE: A MONSTER HOAX

In the 1850s, there was great excitement about a giant serpent which appeared in Silver Lake (New York, USA). People traveled miles to see it and the area became busy and prosperous. But then there was a fire in the local hotel, after which firemen discovered in an attic room the remains of a wire and canvas model of a huge snake. The hotel owner had faked the whole thing to bring more business to his hotel.

STORSJÖN CREATURE

A lake monster from northern Sweden.

For more than 350 years, there have been stories of a huge creature living in Lake Storsjön in northern Sweden. A scientific society exists to investigate life-forms in the lake. According to eyewitnesses, the Storsjön Creature seems to be very like the one from Loch Ness, but is described as having a yellow underbelly.

WHITE RIVER MONSTER

A large beast that lives in White River, Arkansas.

There have supposedly been monsters in the White River since before the American Civil War. One has certainly been reported recently, and eyewitnesses said it was very big and a greyish color with peeling skin. It can walk and it has left huge footprints on the river bank.

SLIMY SLIM

A serpentine lake monster, also known as Sharlie.

Payette Lake (Idaho, USA) is in the mountains and surrounded by forests. Occasional monster stories have been heard over the last 15 years about this quiet lake, and interestingly, the reports are getting more frequent, so the monster is either getting bolder or more careless. The creature has been nicknamed Slimy Slim or Sharlie, and is said to be serpent-like in appearance with a head like that of a crocodile.

Right: Storsjön Creature depicted on a large rune stone.

Beast of
Busco

CHAMP

Lake Champlain's answer to the Loch Ness Monster.

"Champ" was first seen in Lake Champlain (USA/Canada) in the nineteenth century, and the famous showman P. T. Barnum offered $50,000 to anyone who could bring him the body of a dead Champ. The reward was never claimed. Like Nessie, the legend of Champ has become a tourist attraction and lakeside towns and resorts benefit from the story of the creature from the depths. Unlike Nessie, Champ seems to be a huge snake, as none of the 300 or so reports of sightings describes the creature as leaving the water and walking around.

Champ (Lake
Champlain Monster)

BEAST OF BUSCO

A giant snapping turtle.

In 1948 a farmer in Churubusco, Indiana (USA), who had a large pond on his property, started to see fish and waterfowl disappearing from the pond. The cause turned out to be an enormous snapping turtle that some claimed was as big as a large truck. Despite crowds of sightseers turning up to catch a glimpse of it, the monster was never seen again.

CHESSIE

A saltwater monster seen in Chesapeake Bay, USA.

Some witnesses have described "Chessie" as having flippers, but most reports say it is like a large snake or eel, with a head shaped like that of a horse. There have been many sightings of Chessie, and videos and photographs are claimed to show the creature. However, none provides conclusive proof of the monster's existence.

OGOPOGO

Canada's best-known lake monster.

Lake Okanagan in British Columbia (Canada) is a long, narrow, and deep lake very similar to Loch Ness in Scotland. It has its own monster, known as Ogopogo. The most common description of the monster is that it is a serpent, 15–20 ft (5–6 m) long with a horse-like or sheep-like head.

The legend of a monster living in this lake goes back for centuries and there have been many sightings. Originally the monster was known as Natiaka (from a Native American word meaning "lake demon").

One eyewitness account was from 1926. A couple driving past the lake on a very mild day saw the calm lake rippling and looked to see what was causing the movement. They spotted a large, strange-looking animal.

Some experts believe that these serpent-like monsters are a kind of primitive whale, or they may be a variety of sturgeon—a fish that can reach a great size and a great age.

THE DEVIL'S FOOTPRINTS

In February 1855, deep snow lay over the county of South Devon in England. One morning, residents awoke to find a trail of large hoof-prints in the snow, continuing across the countryside for some 60 miles (95 km) and going straight across roofs, walls, and other obstacles. At one point, the prints went down to the estuary of the Exe River and then began again on the other side of the river. As the Devil was believed to have cloven hooves, there were soon stories that he had been seen in person. The tracks never appeared again and have never been explained.

KAPPA

KAPPAS are water goblins that live in rivers and lakes in Japan. They are shaped like humans and are about the size of a nine-year-old child. With scaly skin they are green, yellow, or occasionally blue in color and have webbed hands and feet.

WATER CHILDREN

Kappas, also known as "water children," are not very nice. They cause mischief, entice people into rivers to drown, and are said to kidnap and eat children. In spite of their small size, they're strong and can swim well, and can drag large animals into the water, hold them under and drown them, which is something they like to do. They are particularly fond of attacking horses.

They are really best avoided, but, like many supernatural creatures, they have certain aspects that you can use to your advantage if you have to deal with one. For example, you can buy them off with gifts—they like cucumbers, apparently.

Kappas are said to have a special hole in the top of their heads that contains magical water, which they carry with them when away from water. However, Kappas are also very interested in good manners. So if you meet a Kappa, it's wise to bow very deeply. The Kappa will return the bow, and the water will run out. The Kappa will then lose its power and be unable to move, allowing you to get away safely. Or you could refill the cavity with water, and then the Kappa would have to serve you for eternity.

KELPIE

A magical and dangerous water spirit that looks like a horse.

Kelpies are murderous water-spirits that live in rivers in Scotland and Ireland. A Kelpie usually takes the form of a handsome black horse. It will encourage you to pat it and then to ride it, but once on its back, you will be unable to jump off again. It will gallop into the water with you, pull you down to the depths, and eat you. They like to prey on children in particular.

Sometimes a Kelpie will turn itself into a beautiful woman with long black hair and will make a man fall in love with her, but the end of the story will be the same—he'll drown and be eaten.

It may be useful to know that Kelpies are always very cold to the touch, unlike real horses and women.

POOKA

A shape-shifting trickster spirit that can be deceitful.

Pookas, or Púcas, live around rivers in Scotland, Ireland, and also Wales. They can turn themselves into almost any kind of animal, such a wild horse, but will always have dark fur. They're tricky and like to entice you to go for a ride on their back but, unlike the Kelpie, a Pooka will do you no real harm. They like to deceive and worry humans, and can be destructive if angered, but they can also be friendly and give good advice if treated with respect.

Right: Kelpies take the form of horses or beautiful women.

Ahuitzotl

AHUITZOTL

A nasty water monster from Aztec mythology, the Ahuitzotl lives in rivers in Mexico and Guatemala. It's like a cross between a smooth-haired black dog and a monkey. It has powerful arms and hands and an extra hand at the end of its long tail, which is useful for pulling its victims down into the water. It likes to eat people, especially the eyes, nails, and teeth.

CATOBLEPAS

An African monster that kills with a look, the Catoblepas lives in Ethiopia. It's a large, hairy, buffalo-like creature, which carries its head low and looks at the ground. This is a good thing, because if it raises its head and looks straight at you, you will be turned to stone. Its breath can also kill you.

TARASQUE

There has only ever been one Tarasque, which came out of the Rhône River in Provence, France. It had six feet, a turtle-type shell on its back, and a lion's head. It terrorized the region around the river until it was tamed by Saint Martha. Unfortunately the local people didn't realize that it had been tamed and they killed it. They then regretted what they had done and named their town Tarascon in its memory.

Model of the Tarasque in Tarascon, France.

REVENGE OF THE MULDJEWANGK

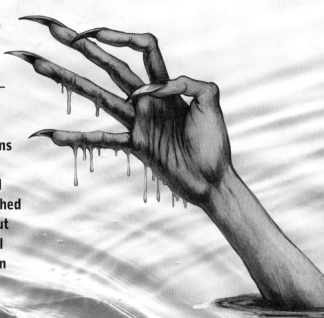

A Muldjewangk is a creature from Australian Aboriginal mythology. It was a huge monster—half-man, half-fish—which lived in the Murray River in South Australia. A Muldjewangk once attacked a steamboat that was owned by Europeans that had some Aboriginal elders on board. As the Muldjewangk's two enormous hands appeared and took hold of the side of the deck, the captain reached for his gun. The elders warned him not to shoot, but he did. The monster went away, but the captain fell ill with terrible blisters all over his body and died in agony six months later.

BUNYIP

The Bunyip is a mysterious creature that is said to be found all over Australia, and is mentioned in the myths of the ancient Dreamtime of the Aboriginal people. It supposedly lives in riverbeds, creeks, or other watery places.

There are many different descriptions of a Bunyip. Some say it's shaggy with a long tail, others describe it as dog-faced; some say it has claws and scaly skin like a crocodile while others report it as having four paws.

What is certain is that a Bunyip lives in or near water and will kill and eat people. All descriptions agree that it has a loud, bellowing cry, which is frightening to hear and serves as a good warning to keep away from the area.

RUSALKA

A beautiful and deadly water ghost.

A Rusalka is the ghost of a young woman or child who has died by drowning. Most Rusalkas were girls who committed suicide because they were betrayed by a lover. They haunt the river where they died (usually in Russia or Poland). They sit by the side of the river in a tree, or they might dance hypnotically in a water-meadow, or sing beautifully on the river bank, but they are bitter and their aim is to capture young men and drown them.

BÄCKAHÄST

The Bäckahäst ("brook horse") is very like a Kelpie, except that it's usually a white horse and appears from the river in foggy weather. To prey on people in boats, it can disguise itself as an upturned boat or a floating log until it gets close to its victims, when it will surge up out of the water, seize them, and drag them down to the depths. It also plays the same trick as the Kelpie, appearing on land as a handsome white horse and persuading unsuspecting children to ride it. Whichever method it uses, the Bäckahäst's aim in life is to drown people and then eat them.

Anyone who climbs on the back of a Bäckahäst, will never be able to get off again.

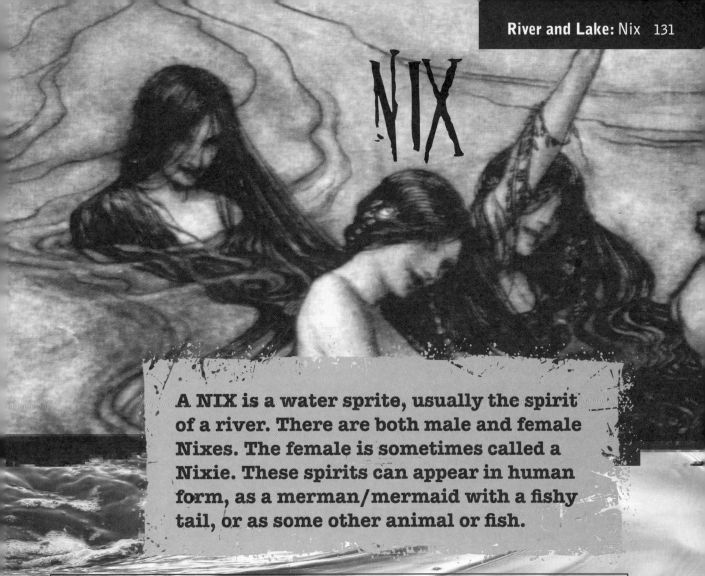

NIX

A NIX is a water sprite, usually the spirit of a river. There are both male and female Nixes. The female is sometimes called a Nixie. These spirits can appear in human form, as a merman/mermaid with a fishy tail, or as some other animal or fish.

DANGEROUS BEAUTIES

Nixes often take the form of either beautiful or old women, and can also become invisible. In many German and Scandinavian folk tales, seeing or hearing a Nix is a sign of danger and death.

Nixes often use song to lure fishermen and sailors into danger. The Lorelei was a famous example. She would sit on a rock in the Rhine River and sing to the boatmen, who would follow her beautiful voice and steer to their deaths on the dangerous rocks nearby. Nixes appear to do things like this purely for their own amusement.

Like other malevolent elves and fairies, Nixes are indifferent to human happiness and can drive a hard bargain. There are stories where a Nix seems friendly and does a favor for a human, but then demands a child in payment. Nixes are said to live in underwater palaces and it is possible to get on their good side by bribing them with gifts.

Some people believe that a Nix takes its power, and even its life, from its particular river and if held captive on land, it will fade away and die.

As well as loving music and dancing, Nixes are thought to be able to tell the future.

SEA
AND
OCEAN

SEA SERPENT

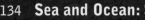

SEA SERPENT

OTHER NAMES: Sea monster.

FACT OR FICTION: Fiction but possibly some sightings were of real, oversized sea creatures, such as an oarfish.

DESCRIPTION: Generally like giant, scaly snakes, up to hundreds of feet long and up to 20 ft (6 m) thick, with heads that are like those of dragons or horses. Some have humps on their back. Some have been said to have hair, shells, eyes that shine, and sometimes a horse-like mane.

WHERE THEY LIVE: In the seas and oceans all around the world.

POWERS: Their immense size and strength makes them very powerful.

WEAKNESSES: Their immense size may make them a little slow-moving. They can only live in water.

DIET: Fish, and other bigger marine creatures such as seals and whales. Sometimes human sailors become part of their diet, too!

A SEA SERPENT is a huge and dangerous creature seen in oceans in many parts of the world. Often hundreds of feet long, these giant sea snakes can attack ships at sea, overturning the boats easily with their huge and powerful bodies. Some people think that sea serpents are probably only whales or other huge fish.

SERPENTS OR FISH?

In the days when a sea voyage could last for years and ships navigated by the stars through uncharted waters, many sailors told tales of giant sea serpents that they'd seen in the far oceans. Like the lake monsters—the Loch Ness Monster and others (see the River & Lake chapter starting on page 118)—the sea serpents had humps on their backs, an undulating movement when swimming, and bony, dragon-like or horse-like heads. They would be seen chasing and eating seals, small whales, and even sharks. The sea serpents were big—so big that any sailors who saw one were worried that it might attack them and cause their ship to overturn.

Modern scientists have suggested that the sea serpents may have been very large sturgeon, or possibly oarfish. Sturgeon are long thin fish that have the right shape of head, but although big, they are not monster-sized. Oarfish are like enormous eels that live at the bottom of the ocean and are very seldom seen. They can grow to at least 15 ft (5 m) long, but even this is considerably smaller than the sea serpents sighted by sailors in the past, and oarfish don't have the distinctive "dragon-like" head so often described.

THE SS TRESCO AND THE SEA SERPENT

Joseph Grey, Second Officer of the SS Tresco, told how, in May 1903 in the South Atlantic, the crew saw a number of sharks swimming past at great speed as if escaping from danger. They then saw something in the water in the direction the sharks had come from.

As it came closer, the sailors could see that it was a huge serpent, about 100 ft (30 m) long, with a narrow, bony head held up out of the water on a long neck. The sailors were terrified that it would attack the Tresco or collide with it. Grey claimed that the creature came close enough so that they could even see drool dripping from its mouth, before it suddenly turned and swam away.

Most people who read the article thought that Grey had simply invented a colorful tale. But then the log of the SS Tresco was discovered. (A ship's log must be an accurate account of everything that happens on board.) It had this entry for May 30, 1903 at 10am, "Passed school of sharks followed by a huge sea monster."

KRAKEN

A KRAKEN is an enormous and aggressive squid that lives at the bottom of the sea. It can attack boats and ships, wrapping its huge tentacles around them and dragging them underwater.

FICTION AND FACT

Sailors in the olden days told tales of the Kraken, a huge octopus or squid, which would surge up from the depths of the ocean, grab onto a ship using the suckers on its many arms, and pull the vessel and everybody on board it down under the water. It would attack without warning and chances of survival for the sailors were slim. The Kraken, thought to be a typical sailors' legend like the mermaid, was said to live in the ocean off the coasts of Norway and Iceland.

Remarkably, we now know that real Krakens exist, although at the other end of the world. The Colossal Squid (Latin name Mesonychoteuthis hamiltoni) has only been known to scientists since 1925. It lives in the deepest water of the Antarctic seas and mature specimens grow to over 40 ft (14 m) long. Colossal Squids have hooks on their eight arms as well as suckers, and are strong enough to pull a sailing-ship underwater. They are rare creatures and are seldom seen in shallow water; they have complex brains and experts say they are probably highly intelligent. During the 1930s there were three reported cases of Colossal Squids attacking ships.

LEVIATHAN

Leviathan is an enormous sea monster that is mentioned several times in the Bible. In the Book of Job the creature is described as being monstrously huge and having terrifying large teeth and scales. It is also said to be able to breathe fire and deflect weapons such as spears. People often think that Leviathan was probably just a huge whale or maybe even a giant crocodile, but what is certain is that it lived in the ocean, not in a river. Often any large sea creature sighted today is referred to as a Leviathan.

Below: Leviathan is often thought to look something like a huge crocodile.

LUSCA

The sea around the islands of the Bahamas is famous for "blue holes"—deep pools and underwater caves that glow blue because of certain minerals in the rocks.

Unfortunately, these beautiful depths are also the home of the Lusca, which is half-shark and half-octopus. Many Bahamians believe that the creature will attack and kill unwary swimmers and divers.

SEA APE

Only one person has ever seen the Sea Ape— the explorer Georg Steller, in 1741 near the Shumagin Islands, Alaska (USA). Steller described it as being around 5 ft (1.5 m) long, having a dog-like head with pointed ears that stuck upward and whiskers, a shark-like tail, and greyish fur on its back but reddish fur on its belly. The way that it rose up out of the water and watched the boat, and its agility, made Steller believe it was some kind of ape. However, it's more likely to have been a seal, especially due to the description of the color, ears, and whiskers.

SCYLLA

SCYLLA was an enormous Greek sea monster with six heads who lurked in a cave, waiting for unsuspecting ships to pass by, which she would then attack, devouring anyone who might be on board.

SIX HEADS

In ancient Greek mythology, Scylla was an immortal and deadly sea monster with six heads, each of which had four eyes and three rows of extremely sharp teeth. She (the monster is female, apparently) also had twelve tentacles instead of legs, and, in some stories, had more toothy heads attached at waist level, which were like the heads of vicious dogs. Scylla waited on the rocks for ships to come near enough for her to snatch the sailors and devour them.

BEAUTY AND BEAST

According to the ancient Roman writer Ovid, Scylla was originally a beautiful nymph. One day she was seen by the sea god, Glaucus, and he fell in love with her. However, Scylla did not return his affection and she ran from him, onto land where he could not follow. Wishing to find a spell to make her fall in love with him, Glaucus sought out the witch, Circe. Unfortunately, Circe fell in love with Glaucus and decided to get rid of Scylla. She transformed the nymph into the sea monster.

CHARYBDIS

Another ancient Greek monster of the sea who creates dangerous whirlpools.

Charybdis is an evil monster who can create powerful and dangerous whirlpools. Also a female monster, she is like an enormous bladder with flippers, and she swallows a huge amount of sea water and then vomits it back out to form whirlpools that cause ships to sink. It is assumed that Charybdis eats the sailors, and the ships too.

"BETWEEN SCYLLA AND CHARYBDIS"

The Greek legend is that these two monsters live on either side of a strait, or narrow channel of water, and work in partnership. Sailors who steer their ship away from one will be caught by the other. So, the expression "to be between Scylla and Charybdis" means to be caught between two bad things and unable to avoid either of them.

MERMAID

MERMAID

OTHER NAMES: Merman.

FACT OR FICTION: Fiction.

DESCRIPTION: About the same size as a human but half-woman (or man) and half-fish. The human half (from the waist up) of the mermaid is that of a beautiful young woman with long hair, and the bottom half is long and scaly with a fish-like tail.

WHERE THEY LIVE: Under the sea, sometimes in beautiful palaces of coral, decorated with pearls.

POWERS: Some mermaids can sing beautiful songs that lure human men into the sea. Powerful swimmers. One Chinese mermaid was said to be able to create priceless pearls from her tears.

WEAKNESSES: Having fish tails, they can only survive in the sea and not venture onto land.

DIET: Fish.

OTHER: Seeing a mermaid is sometimes thought of as an omen of bad luck, especially to sailors, for whom it often means the approach of bad weather.

A MERMAID is half-woman, half -fish, usually beautiful with long shining hair and with a lovely singing voice. The word "mermaid" is made up of the words "mere" (which was the Old English word for "sea") and "maid," meaning a young woman.

MERFOLK

There are many stories of mermaids from around the world. Mermen—half-men, half-fish—are less often talked about, but do appear in some stories.

Both mermaids and mermen can be serious trouble for human beings. Mermaids are extremely vain and spend time combing their hair and admiring their own reflection. Often you hear a mermaid's voice before you see her. They sing beautifully, and their song, once heard, will haunt you forever.

People are fascinated by mermaids, and mermaids are fascinated by people, and that's where the danger is. The typical mermaid story tells of a man falling in love with a mermaid who takes him down to her home under the sea—where, of course, he drowns. Some say that mermaids are simply not very smart and don't realize that humans can't breathe under water, while others believe that mermaids actually delight in charming foolish men and leading them to their doom. But mermaids can also fall in love with human men and follow them onto land. Obviously then, things become very difficult for a mermaid because she can't walk. Different stories tell of mermaids desperately trying to hide their tails, or even striking a terrible bargain with some magician so that they can walk, but only at the cost of extreme pain. In any case, these love affairs never end well and often lead to the death of the mermaid.

AN UNCONVINCING SCIENTIFIC EXPLANATION

Scientists have attempted to explain mermaid legends by saying that what the sailors actually saw was a seal, sea cow, or more likely, a manatee. These gentle, slow-moving water mammals do have tails and do sometimes sit on rocks and watch passing ships, but that's where the resemblance ends. They are grey with big snouts and tiny, far apart eyes. It's hard to believe that many sailors through the ages could have mistaken them for beautiful mermaids.

A **SIREN** is a creature that is part bird, part woman, who likes to sit on rocky islands in the sea, luring sailors to their death on the treacherous rocks with her lovely singing voice.

SIREN

FATAL SONG

Sirens are sometimes confused with mermaids, but they are not the same. A Siren may look like a beautiful woman, or she may be part bird, part woman. Where Sirens and mermaids are alike is that they both have spell-binding singing voices. Sirens sing in a hypnotic way, which makes people follow the song, even if it leads them to destruction.

Sirens appear in ancient Greek mythology, where they live on rocky islands and sing until sailors, trying to get close to them, steer their ships onto the rocks. Only the deaf or the very intelligent will escape.

ODYSSEUS AND THE SIREN

Odysseus wanted both to sail safely past the island of the Sirens and to hear what they sounded like. He made all his crew block their ears with wax, while he kept his ears open, but made the sailors tie him tightly to the ship's mast. As they reached the island, he heard the Sirens' beautiful song and was unable to resist. He begged his sailors to untie him so that he could jump off the ship and try to reach the singers. Luckily, the men couldn't hear what he was saying.

DAVY JONES

**The legendary Devil
of the deep blue sea.**

To go to Davy Jones's Locker means to
drown. No one knows where the name "Davy
Jones" came from, but every sailor certainly
knows who he is. He may look and behave
like a pirate, or he may appear more like
his cousin the Devil, with horns and a tail,
but either way Davy Jones is a dark and evil
force, as dangerous and unpredictable as the
deep sea itself. A light-hearted pantomime
version of Davy appears in the traditional
ritual of "crossing the line" (crossing the
Equator) on board ships. But the real Davy
Jones is not spoken about very much. It's
better not to mention him, because "talk of
the Devil and he'll appear."

ASPIDOCHELONE

**Is it an island? Or is
it a sea monster?**

The hard-to-pronounce Aspidochelone (a
Greek name meaning "asp turtle") may be a
huge whale or some kind of enormous turtle.
It is certainly very large, because when it
floats on the surface of the sea—as it often
does—the crews of passing ships mistake it
for an island. They anchor their ship nearby,
row "ashore" in boats and walk around on
the monster's back. All is well until they start
lighting a fire, and then disaster strikes as
the monster dives. Aspidochelone is
generally considered to be quite evil.

GHOST SHIP

GHOST SHIP

OTHER NAMES: Phantom ship.

FACT OR FICTION: The type of ghost ship with a crew of ghosts is fiction. But the type of ghost ship that is discovered sailing with no crew is fact.

DESCRIPTION: Usually just a regular-looking ship but sometimes they can be surrounded by an eerie ghostly light.

WHERE THEY LIVE: At sea.

POWERS: They don't actually have any special powers, but seeing one is a sign of doom.

FAMOUS GHOST SHIPS: The Flying Dutchman (see opposite), the Caleuche (a mythical ghost ship from Chile), the Lady Lovibond (a ship wrecked in 1748, which appears off the coast of Kent in England, every 50 years), the Eliza Battle (an American paddle steamer that caught fire at the end of the nineteenth century, which appears now and then in flames as a warning of disaster), the Marie Celeste (see opposite), the Carroll Deering (a cargo ship that ran aground in 1921 and was found completely abandoned with no sign of crew).

THERE ARE TWO KINDS of ghost ships—those that sail the seas with a crew of ghosts, and those that are found drifting with not a soul on board, and no sign of where the crew or passengers went. Seeing either kind of ghost ship is considered to be extremely unlucky.

HAUNTED SHIPS WITH A CREW OF GHOSTS

The most famous of this type of ghost ship is the Flying Dutchman. This ship eternally sails the seas, appearing suddenly and silently mid-ocean. If another ship tries to communicate, its sailors will reply, sending messages to people who are long dead. One legend is that the captain, or possibly the whole crew, of the Flying Dutchman once committed a terrible crime and are sailing the oceans forever as punishment. Another story is that the captain was once trying to sail the ship around the Cape of Good Hope in terrible winds. He swore that he would be eternally damned if he didn't get around the Cape that night. The ship was lost, and doomed to carry out his threat forever. Many sailors have seen the ship, including the future King George V of England who supposedly saw it off the coast of Australia in 1880.

SHIPS WITH NO CREW

The most famous of these is the Marie Celeste. This merchant ship was found in the Atlantic Ocean on December 4, 1872. The ship was clean and in good condition, the sails were hoisted, and the ship was making good speed toward Gibraltar. There were enough supplies of food and water for six months in the stores. The belongings of the crew and passengers were all untouched. However, there was not a single person on board. There was no sign of violence or a struggle. One lifeboat was missing, but no one who had been on the ship was ever seen or heard of again.

TALOS

TALOS was a bronze giant of ancient Greek myth who lived on the island of Crete. His job was to guard the princess Europa, who lived on the island, and to ward off any invaders or pirates. He had molten lead in his single vein.

BRONZE GIANT

The giant Talos, from ancient Greek mythology, was made entirely of bronze. He may have been a living giant, but was more likely a kind of animated statue or robot. In some stories he had bronze wings. Talos was fierce and dangerous, and was the guardian of the island of Crete, and he walked or flew all the way around the coast of the island three times every day, watching for pirates or other invaders. If any ship came near, he would throw huge rocks at it. He was put onto Crete to guard the princess Europa, who had been taken to the island by Zeus,

the king of the gods, who was in love with her, and who had abducted Europa and placed her on this island.

Talos's bronze body came in useful at times. He could jump into a fire and heat himself until he was red hot, so that he could then clasp his enemies in a murderous, scorching hug. He was finally destroyed by the enchantress Medea, who first hypnotized him with the help of some evil spirits. She then removed a plug from his ankle, which allowed the liquid metal that he had instead of blood, to run out onto the ground. The bronze giant bled to death.

CYCLOPS

A CYCLOPS is an extremely strong and bad-tempered giant of ancient Greek and Roman legend, who only had one terrifying eye in the middle of his forehead. The word "cyclops" probably means "round eye."

ONE-EYED MONSTERS

The Cyclopes were legendary giants. Each Cyclops had only one eye in the middle of his forehead. Cyclopes lived a very long time, were immensely strong, even for giants, and were well-known for their terrible tempers and generally grouchy dispositions.

Cyclopes were often blacksmiths, but the most famous Cyclops is Polyphemus, who was a shepherd and lived on an island with his own herd of giant sheep. He captured the great Greek traveller Odysseus (from Homer's epic tale, *The Odyssey*) and his companions when they landed on the island and wandered into his cave by accident.

To the captive travelers' horror, Polyphemus began killing and eating them, two for each meal, and no amount of persuasion would change his intention to eat them all. Finally, Odysseus managed to trick Polyphemus into getting very drunk, and then blinded his eye using a stick of wood. But even blind, Polyphemus was dangerous, and the Greeks only escaped him by hiding among his big sheep when he let the flock out in the morning.

The enraged and blinded Polyphemus called on Poseidon, the sea god, for revenge, and Poseidon sent wild storms to threaten Odysseus and his companions as they continued their voyage.

THE
SKIES

EXTRA-TERRESTRIAL

OTHER NAMES: Alien, Martian, Little Green Man.

FACT OR FICTION: So far, science has not discovered any planet on which life (as we know it) could occur. But fiction is full of extra-terrestrial visitors and there are many real-life stories of "close encounters."

DESCRIPTION: Aliens encountered on Earth have often (but not always) been described as child-sized and pale grey, with large dark eyes.

WHERE THEY LIVE: None of the planets near to Earth is capable of supporting life. Extra-terrestrials must therefore live on distant planets, as yet undiscovered.

POWERS: It is often assumed that aliens are more advanced life-forms than humans. They are sometimes credited with telepathic powers.

WEAKNESSES: Some aliens appear to be physically small and spindly with little bodily strength.

DIET: We know very little about what aliens might eat or drink.

OTHER CHARACTERISTICS: Travel in spaceships, "flying saucers," or Unidentified Flying Objects (UFOs). Often interested in studying humans and have been reported to take people away to do experiments on them.

EXTRA-TERRESTRIALS are creatures from outer space or another planet. The word "extra-terrestrial" is Latin for "outside Earth." Although science fiction books, movies, and television shows are full of extra-terrestrials, there are many supposed real-life sightings of Little Green Men.

ROSWELL

In 1947, some kind of unusual craft fell from the air at night and crashed near Roswell in New Mexico, USA. It was described in the local paper as a "flying saucer," but the official explanation was that it had been a weather balloon. After the initial excitement the event was largely forgotten.

In the late 1970s, however, rumors began to circulate that the craft or UFO had indeed been a spaceship, with aliens on board who had been killed or injured in the crash, and that the authorities were covering this up. An ex-army officer who had been involved in clearing the crash site stated that in his opinion the craft did not originate from planet Earth.

More rumors over the next 10 years were followed by the claim from a former army scientist that bodies of aliens had been kept frozen in a top-secret morgue and autopsies (post-mortems) had been carried out on them.

The creatures were described as small and silver with very large eyes. There was even some film footage which, it was claimed, showed one of these autopsies taking place—though this was later shown to be fake. However, the U.S. military and government have always denied that any aliens were captured at Roswell.

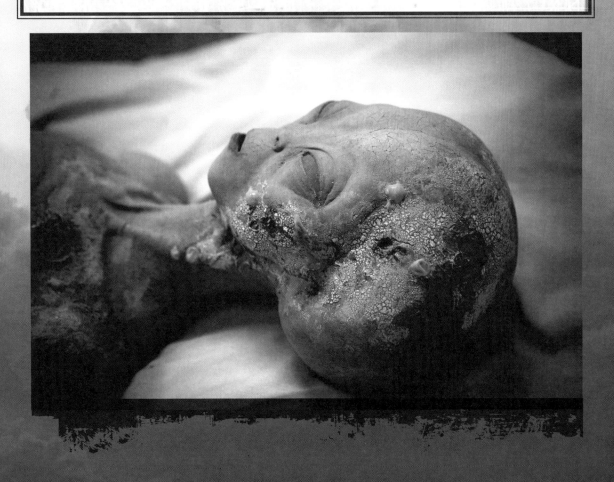

FLATWOODS MONSTER

Many residents of Flatwoods, West Virginia, USA, saw a big glowing orange object fall from the sky on September 12, 1952. They also smelled an unpleasant odor that was like burning metal.

On the same night, several people claimed to have encounters with monstrous creatures. They all described the creatures as about 10 ft (3 m) tall, human-shaped but with bulging non-human eyes, and wearing some sort of draped skirt-like garment. They seemed to give off a pungent-smelling mist. The creatures made a hissing noise at the witnesses but didn't attack, instead moving off toward where the glowing object had landed. The witnesses were paralyzed with fear and they were all ill after the encounters, with vomiting and sore throats, which they thought were caused by the mist.

One interesting fact of this case is that the different witnesses all independently came up with similar descriptions of the monsters, which they had met in different places.

Scientists have suggested that the orange object was a meteor, but that would not explain the creatures. Another possible explanation is that it was some kind of experimental aircraft carrying chemical weapons, which crash-landed, and that the "monsters" were actually just pilots in protective suits. Or, of course, they were actually aliens.

HOPKINSVILLE GOBLIN

In 1955, in the area around Hopkinsville, Kentucky, USA, there were a number of sightings of UFOs with flashing lights. These were seen by police and other reliable witnesses.

Two families in the area then had encounters with small, grey humanoid creatures with long claws on their fingers, glowing eyes, and big pointed ears. Unlike many reported aliens, they seemed to be aggressive and even malicious. They scratched at the windows and doors of the families' houses and climbed onto the roofs.

The Sutton family shot at them with rifles but were unable to wound them—there was just a sound as if the bullet had hit a piece of metal. The creatures seemed to be able to fly or float and used their legs very little. After some time, the terrified Suttons made a break for it and drove to the local police station. The police came back to the house but found nothing unusual.

Both families were sensible people and the police were sure it was not a hoax. The mystery has never been solved.

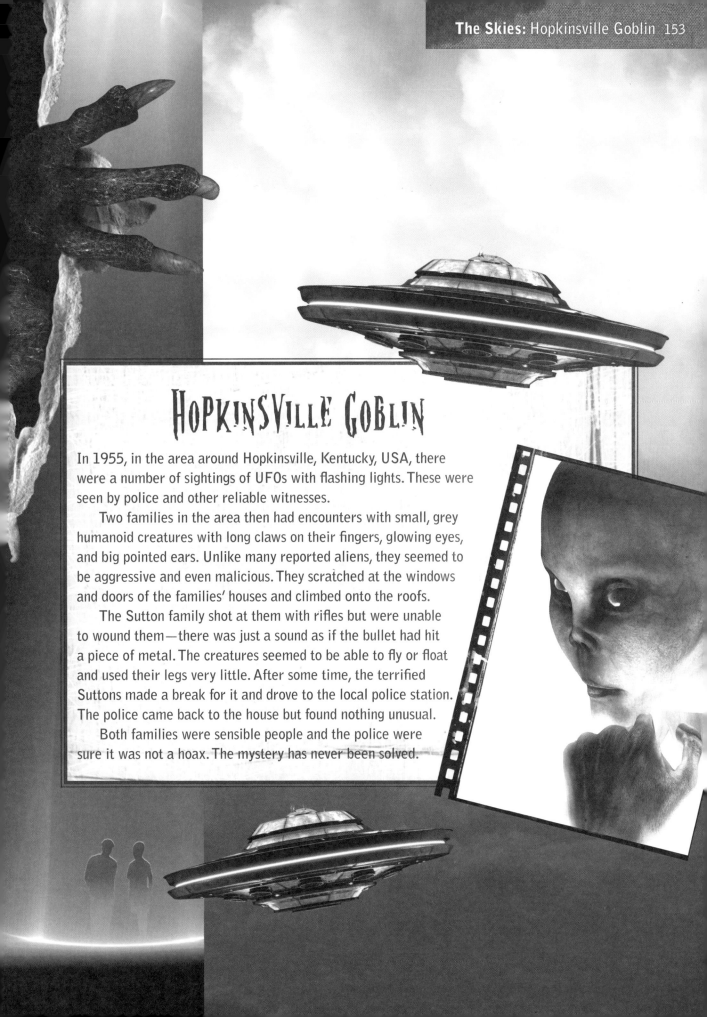

GREMLIN

A destructive imp that specializes in damaging aircraft.

Probably a relative of the Boggart and the Poltergeist, the Gremlin loves to cause damage to machinery. It particularly likes to sabotage aircraft, and in fact pilots in the British Royal Air Force were the first to establish the existence of Gremlins. They suspected that repeated damage to aircraft couldn't just be explained by bad luck or a careless mechanic—something was actually sabotaging their planes. Seeing teeth marks on frayed cables really made them wonder!

MOTHMAN

A flying man who is a harbinger of doom.

The Mothman was seen by a number of people in Point Pleasant, West Virginia, USA, in 1966–67, and, according to some reports, has been seen occasionally since then. He is described as 7 ft (2.15 m) tall with red, glowing eyes and huge wings, with a wingspan of maybe 10 ft (3 m).

Although the Mothman will not hurt you, seeing him is a sign that something very bad is going to happen, and anyone who sees him gains an extra ability to foretell what the upcoming bad event will be.

There is a convincing theory that the Mothman is actually just a large heron, but Point Pleasant celebrates him with an annual Mothman Festival every September.

GRIFFIN

A majestic and ferocious mythical beast, half lion and half eagle.

The Griffin, or Gryphon, has the body, back, legs, and tail of a lion and the head, front legs, and wings of an eagle. It also has little pointed ears, but these are the only charming things about a Griffin, which is a big scary monster built for battle and destruction. It has long talons on its eagle-type front feet and a huge sharp beak, plus all the strength of a lion. Do not, on any account, annoy a Griffin.

For some reason, Griffins hate horses, and horses feel the same about Griffins. Given the chance, a Griffin will kill and eat any horse it happens to meet.

On the other hand, Griffins love gold, which they collect and hoard.

HIPPOGRIFF

A cross between a Griffin and a horse.

Strangely, given that Griffins hate horses, the two beasts are the parents of the Hippogriff (also spelled Hippogryph). This legendary monster has the eagle head and wings of a Griffin, a lion-like body, and the back legs of a horse. Not surprisingly, Hippogriffs have a reputation for being mixed-up, wild, and treacherous. Because of the hostility between horses and Griffins, Hippogriffs are also very, very rare.

Thunderbird

In Native American legend, the Thunderbird is a huge bird with great magical and spiritual powers. The beat of its wings causes the thunder and the lightning flashes from its eyes. In some stories, the Thunderbird is a messenger for the Great Spirit. In other tales, it's more of a trickster spirit and can disguise itself as another creature and even as a human being.

Left: The eagle-like Roc.
Below: The Native American Thunderbird.

Roc

The Roc or Rukh is a creature of Arabian legend. It's like an eagle, but enormous—big and powerful enough to prey on elephants. A Roc will seize an elephant in its huge claws and fly up into the air with it. It then drops the elephant from a great height so that it smashes to death, whereupon the Roc flies back down to the earth and devours it.

Ahool

Named after its unnerving cry, the Ahool is a huge bat that is said to fly through the rainforests of Java. It has a face like a monkey and vast leathery wings, with a wingspan of 10 ft (3 m).

WYVERN

THE WYVERN is like a small, flying dragon. It is a scaly creature with wings and a long, spiked tail. It is more bird-like in shape than a dragon, as it has a beak and only two legs, and its wings are bigger in proportion to its size.

FLYING SERPENT

The name "Wyvern" comes from an Anglo-Saxon word for a snake, and there have been tales of Wyverns in Britain and Northern Europe for many centuries. Wyverns were believed to be creatures of evil, even messengers of the Devil, and some said that they spread the Plague. Though smaller than Dragons—they're sometimes called Dragonets—Wyverns are aggressive and nasty.

Although Wyverns are hard to fight since they are good fliers, the females are supposed to be particularly tricky to deal with.

A rare variation is the Sea Wyvern, which has a fishy tail like that of a Mermaid.

The Wyvern was used as a symbol of battle and conquest, and perhaps for this reason, despite being so unpleasant, Wyverns were often used in heraldry as part of a "coat of arms" and are still very popular as symbols, badges, or mascots for sports clubs, towns, schools, etc.

Some cryptozoologists (experts that specialize in animals that are said to exist but haven't been found) think Wyverns might be surviving dinosaurs (pterosaurs) that lived 65 million years ago.

MAORI BIRD WOMAN

**In Maori legend, Kurangaituku the Bird Woman
is a ferocious giantess with long claws.**

The Maori Bird Woman captured the hunter Hatupatu and kept him as a pet, but he got away from her by hiding inside a rock. When he thought it was safe to come out, he emerged from the rock, noticing the terrible claw marks the Bird Woman had angrily left in it. But Kurangaituku was waiting and pursued him. He led her towards the hot springs of Whakarewarewa and managed to fool her into stepping into the scalding water. Kurangaituku was boiled to death. The rock with the claw marks can still be seen, at a place called Atiamuri.

STRIX

**An evil owl with an appetite for human flesh, the Strix
was a monster of ancient Greek and Roman mythology.**

The Strix was a kind of huge owl, which ate people, tearing them limb from limb. It was obviously very big for an owl, and it could plunge down from the night sky and attack you, first drinking your blood before it ate your flesh. In ancient Greek, "strix" originally meant just "owl," but if you talked about the Strix, people knew that you were talking about the monster, and shuddered with fear.

THE WILD HUNT

THE WILD HUNT is made up of ghostly warriors, horses, and hounds that wildly pursue an unseen victim through the night sky. The Wild Hunt is usually seen in December or early January, at dead of night.

SPECTERS IN THE SKY

Some say the Wild Hunt can only be seen between Christmas and the Twelfth Night (January 6). Sometimes it gallops high in the sky and sometimes you can meet it on a country road, as it hurtles along just above the ground.

A ghostly light surrounds the Hunt. The riders are fierce and wild, their horses tall and powerful, and their hounds huge and ferocious with glowing eyes. They move at terrifying speed and you can't usually see what they're chasing. In Scandinavia, it's called Odin's Hunt and is believed to be led by Odin, one of the greatest of the ancient gods. In some parts of England they believe that King Arthur leads the Hunt with his Knights of the Round Table. In other places they say that the riders are led by Herne the Hunter, a god of the forest resembling a giant man with antlers on his head.

Seeing the Wild Hunt is often a sign that bad things are going to happen somewhere, but with any luck, if you get out of its way, you won't be harmed.

If you are nice to the Wild Hunt, or help them in any way, you might be placed under a protective spell or you might be given riches.

THE
DESERT

MUMMY

MUMMY

FACT OR FICTION: Mummified bodies are fact, but the idea of monstrous mummies rising from the dead and attacking people is purely fiction.

DESCRIPTION: A mummy is always wrapped in linen bandages. Usually these are dirty, tattered and torn, and sometimes unravel, revealing the mummy's body and rotting flesh.

WHERE THEY LIVE: The most famous real mummies are from Egypt, but there are also mummies in South America, China, New Guinea, Australia, and Europe.

POWERS: A mummy is tremendously strong, and resistant to bullets, knives, sticks, and stones—mainly because it's already dead. It can possess the mind or body of a living person.

WEAKNESSES: Can't resist fire, so burning a mummy is the best way to get rid of one. Some ancient spells can be effective too.

OTHER CHARACTERISTICS: Dead mummies can be brought to life by conducting a ritual or reciting a spell or incantation.

WRAPPED IN TATTERED BANDAGES, the mummy rises from its ancient Egyptian tomb to haunt, terrify, and sometimes kill people. It may seek revenge against those who disturbed it or against the descendants of its ancient enemies. Or it may try to raise a long-lost loved one from the dead, while murdering anyone who gets in its way.

PRESERVING THE DEAD

Mummification is the process of treating, or embalming, a dead body so that it will not rot. It was most famously practiced by the ancient Egyptians, but was used in other parts of the world too. Animals can also be mummified.

In ancient Egypt, the process involved covering the body in salt to dry it out then rubbing the skin with oils or resin to keep it flexible. The body was then stuffed with a filling such as sand or sawdust and wrapped in linen bandages to stop the air getting to it. Finally, the corpse was sealed inside a strong coffin, or sarcophagus, and placed within a tomb. The dry desert air would also help preserve the body.

A SMALL BAG OF MUMMY, PLEASE

People in the Middle Ages believed that mummies contained a magical tar-like substance called bitumen, which could heal a variety of diseases (the word "mummy" actually comes from the Arabic mumiyah, meaning "bitumen"). As a result, many ancient Egyptian corpses were ground up into a powder called "mummy" that was sold all over Europe. When traders ran out of Egyptian mummies, they sneakily started using the bodies of criminals. This practice continued until the eighteenth century.

CURSE OF THE MUMMY

From ancient times, it was said that anyone who opened the tomb of a pharaoh would suffer bad luck forever after, and a number of tombs actually contained written warnings, such as "Cursed be those who disturb the rest of a Pharaoh." From the eighteenth century onward, several explorers and archaeologists reported bad things happening to them after entering tombs, including illnesses, accidents, and mummies haunting their dreams.

Soon after a British expedition led by Howard Carter opened the tomb of Egyptian pharaoh Tutankhamen in 1922, several members of the party were struck by misfortune. The expedition's sponsor, Lord Carnarvon, got a mosquito bite on his left cheek and died of blood poisoning—spookily, the body of Tutankhamen was said to have a wound in the same place. Others also died of fevers or blood diseases, or were murdered or committed suicide.

A story even circulated that on the day Carter entered the tomb his house was broken into and his canary eaten by a cobra —the symbol of ancient Egyptian rulers. Carter, however, lived for another 17 years, dying at the age of 64.

Below: Howard Carter examining the mummy of King Tutankhamen in 1922.

THE UNDEAD

Mummies are often considered to be "undead" in their tomb, and some people attempt to bring them back to life to serve them as their own personal monster to fight their enemies. A mummy may be brought back to life by performing a ritual or reciting an ancient spell. Sometimes tomb robbers or archaeologists do this unwittingly by reading out inscriptions they find in a tomb. Even before they have finished speaking, the sarcophagus starts to open and a bandaged hand reaches out and then they are in trouble! However, if you're lucky, as soon as the mummy is exposed to air, it may disintegrate.

If you unleash a mummy by mistake and don't know what you're doing, controlling it can be a challenging business. Reburying it might work if you can first immobilize it, but there's no guarantee that it won't be dug up again later. Sometimes reciting another spell will cause a mummy to become mortal and quickly age and die. But burning it to ashes is usually a swifter and surer way.

CHIMERA

Dreaded by the ancient Greeks, this deadly, fire-breathing creature is three sinister beasts rolled into one.

A Chimera has the forelegs, shoulders, and head of a lion, the body of a goat with a goat's head on its back, and the tail of a dragon with a serpent's head at its end. The Chimera is thought to have emerged from the mountain of the same name in southwestern Turkey, where, to this day, vents in the ground spout fountains of burning gas. A famous Greek myth tells how a Chimera devastated that region before being killed by the hero Bellephon.

BASILISK

Said to be the king of serpents, the Basilisk is a deadly snake with a crown-like crest on its head.

The Basilisk was first reported in the deserts of Libya in ancient times, and was widely feared in Europe in the Middle Ages. So powerful is its venom that even its breath or hiss is fatal; worse still, it can kill you just by looking at you—in fact, the only way to study one safely is by observing its reflection in a mirror. The weasel is the only creature that can kill a Basilisk, and it does this by using its powerful smell. Strangely, Basilisks are also afraid of chickens, which medieval travelers would often carry for protection in Basilisk-infested realms.

COCKATRICE

The fearsome dragon-like Cockatrice is often confused with the Basilisk, and some say it is the same creature.

Like the Basilisk, the Cockatrice can kill with just a bite or a look. But although it has the tail of a serpent, the Cockatrice has the head of a cockerel, several legs, and strong wings. And, whereas a Basilisk is born when a cockerel incubates the egg of a serpent or toad, a Cockatrice is brought to life when a toad or serpent hatches the egg of a cockerel.

Below: The Cockatrice is similar to the Basilisk but it has legs and the head of a cockerel.

AMPHISBAENA

With a head and poisonous fangs at either end of its body, this venomous snake spells double trouble.

Native to the deserts of North Africa, the Amphisbaena is said to have been born from the spilled blood of the famous snake-haired Gorgon of Greek mythology, Medusa. In medieval imagery, it is sometimes depicted with a lizard-like body, the legs of a chicken, and feathered wings. Though dangerous, it is believed to have medicinal benefits: wearing an Amphisbaena skin around your neck might not look or smell great, but it is said to cure arthritis and the common cold.

EVIL GENIE

EVIL GENIE

OTHER NAMES: Djinn, jinn, jinni.

FACT OR FICTION: Most experts would say fiction, but many spooked desert travelers would argue otherwise.

DESCRIPTION: An invisible spirit that can make itself visible in different forms. It may appear as a dragon, snake, dog, or other animal, or as a human. Modern depictions usually show a genie as a large, strong man wearing traditional Arabian clothes.

WHERE THEY LIVE: Everywhere—but you can't see them! Most often reported in North Africa, the Middle East, and Asia

POWERS: Can assume the form of a human or any animal, move at great speed and fly, make objects move, whip up winds and sandstorms, and conjure false images.

WEAKNESSES: Magicians can call up genies and, if particularly skilled, can control them at will. But this is fraught with risk, since dangerous, vengeful genies are hard for even the greatest wizards to control.

OTHER CHARACTERISTICS: If you're lucky enough to run into a friendly genie on a good day, it might just grant you a wish, or three.

THANKS TO MODERN stories and movies, we tend to think of genies as friendly spirits, ever ready to grant three life-enhancing wishes. But the true genies of Arabic myth, the djinns, are fallen gods or demons, determined to cause mischief and destruction.

OUT OF NOWHERE

Born from fire, genies are supernatural spirits that dwell invisibly all over the world —in fire, water, earth, air, trees, rocks, and old buildings. If disturbed by someone, they may exact swift and terrible revenge. Travelers in the deserts of North Africa and Arabia especially fear disturbing genies, as evil ones will then take great delight in making sure they get lost and never find their way home again. Such genies might even create false images of water, oases, fruit, and palaces—mirages, in other words —or appear as friendly humans in order to mislead their prey. Some genies will even kill and eat their victims.

LURKING IN A LAMP

The most famous stories about genies appear in the medieval collection of Arabic and Asian folktales known as *The Thousand and One Nights* (or *The Arabian Nights*). In perhaps the best-known tale, *Aladdin's Wonderful Lamp*, Aladdin, a poor young Chinese boy, retrieves an old oil lamp from a cave and finds that by rubbing it he can summon genies that will grant his every wish. Repelling attempts by evil sorcerers to steal the lamp, he becomes wealthy, happy, and powerful and marries the Emperor's beautiful daughter.

SPHINX

PART LION, PART HUMAN, the Sphinx is familiar as a temple guardian and royal symbol of ancient Egypt. But the Sphinx of Greek myth is far more terrifying—an evil, sinister creature with the head of a woman, a lion's body, a snake's tail, and the wings of an eagle.

EGYPTIAN SPHINX

Ancient Egyptian Sphinxes usually have the body of a lion and the head of a human, most often a man. Many pharaohs had statues of Sphinxes carved with likenesses of their own face or symbol. The most famous is the Great Sphinx, an enormous statue near the Great Pyramids of Giza.

THE RIDDLE OF THE SPHINX

In ancient Greek stories, the Sphinx gained its different physical features and came to be seen as nasty and unpleasant. In Thebes, a Sphinx would pose a riddle to young men visiting the city —'What creature walks on four legs, then two, then three?'—and strangle and devour them when they failed to answer correctly. Finally, the traveler Oedipus gave the correct response—"The human, who first crawls on all fours, then walks on two legs, then walks with a cane in old age"—and the horrified Sphinx threw herself to her death from the city walls.

In medieval times, the Sphinx was also said to guard the secrets and treasures of great sorcerers.

YOWIE

A legendary creature of the Australian outback, the Yowie is a hairy, ape-like beast standing up to 6½ ft (2 m) tall.

Aboriginal myths speak of "ape-men" inhabiting remote deserts, forests, and mountains, mainly in eastern Australia. In the nineteenth century many European settlers claimed that such creatures had savaged their livestock. Yowies are said to be so strong that they can rip the heads off bulls, run fast enough to outpace any human— despite the fact that their large feet point backwards—and smell disgusting. Sightings are still reported regularly all over Australia.

MONGOLIAN DEATH WORM

In the deserts of Mongolia, locals speak of a colossal red worm that sprays victims with a lethal, acidic venom.

Thought to hibernate under the sand for most of the year and only become active in June and July, the Mongolian death worm is bright red, up to 5 ft (1.5 m) long, and looks like a massive earthworm. Not only can it kill with its poison, but touching one will also bring instant death, and it can send out deadly lightning-like electrical charges. Several recent expeditions have searched for the worm, but no specimens—alive or dead—have yet been found.

Mongolian Death Worm

MAGIC
AND
CHARMS

SPELLS AND HEXES

SPELLS are magical words that control people or things, such as turning them into another creature, making them act a certain way, or even killing them. Spells may not always be evil, and can sometimes be cast to make good things happen, like falling in love or getting well. However, hexes, jinxes, and curses are definitely not good.

GOOD AND BAD SPELLS

The most reliable sign that someone has magical ability—whether good or evil—is their ability to cast hexes and spells. If you can cast a spell on someone or something, you can make that person or thing do what you want. So, for instance, you can make somebody go cross-eyed or turn them into a rabbit, or you can cause normal food to suddenly give acute indigestion to everybody who eats it.

If you have even more power, you can command the weather. More seriously still, you can make your enemies go mad or die a terrible death. Only one exact combination of words, with perhaps the mixing of special ingredients to be burned or eaten, will achieve the required effect. Witches and wizards spend their lives learning these formulas, acquiring spells of increasing power as they get older, until they're very ancient and know some extremely dangerous and powerful spells.

For those of us who are not witches or wizards, the best thing is to know something about spells, so that we have some idea what to do if we should ever find ourselves under a spell for whatever reason.

INCANTATIONS

An incantation is the words of a spell, which usually must be said aloud a set number of times for the spell to take effect.

The moon is often important when casting spells. A spell cast at full moon will be more powerful. A spell to get rid of something or someone will work better when the moon is "waning"(fading), while a spell to summon something or someone will be more suited to the "waxing" (growing) moon.

Symbols are frequently used in spells, whether they're drawn on the floor or on a piece of paper which may be burned as the spell is cast. Typical symbols used are the pentagram, hexagram, and spiral.

POTIONS

Potions are spells that are magically contained in drinks. They can have strong or lesser effects. If taken by accident, they are usually difficult to counteract and have to be allowed to wear off.

HEXES AND JINXES

A hex is usually a spell of general misfortune. The word comes from the German "Hexe," meaning witch. If someone has a hex put on them, from that moment on nothing will go right in their lives.

A jinx is like a hex, but not as bad, often causing someone to fail in a sport or at work. Many people believe that, even without magic knowledge, you can accidentally put a jinx on a sports player or team if you talk over-confidently about how well they'll play.

BLACK MAGIC

BLACK MAGIC is generally unfriendly magic, and involves enchantments in connection with death, damage, and destruction. Obviously only evil witches and wizards use this type of magic.

NASTY STUFF

Black magic is dangerous stuff and should be avoided by anyone with good sense. It often involves using the spirits or bodies of the dead to harm the living. It can be used to bring illness, bad luck, unhappiness, madness, or death to someone who is the enemy of the magician.

Like most magic, it cuts both ways: you can't cast a powerful black magic spell without also harming yourself. Those who use black magic can persuade themselves that they're strong enough to handle it, but they will almost certainly be wrong. A powerful magician may be able to summon up a demon to carry out a murderous errand for him, but the price to be paid may be very high indeed —his soul, for example.

TYPES OF MAGIC

Magic spells and rituals are categorized according to the purpose for which they are used:

- Black magic is for damage, destruction, and death.
- White magic is for healing and good luck.
- Green magic is used to make things grow and to attract money.
- Red magic is for love and passion.
- Purple magic is for gaining power.

TUPILAK

A TUPILAK is a kind of "devil doll" that is used in traditional Inuit culture to bring harm to an enemy. Inuit magicians would make a carved doll to carry their curses and bad wishes to their enemies. It was believed that sometimes an evil spirit would take control of the doll.

DEVIL DOLL

The Inuits, who were once known as Eskimos, are the native peoples of the Arctic region of North America and Europe.

Inuit magicians would make a Tupilak doll at night, in absolute secrecy, creating it out of parts of animals and adding more spells at each stage over several nights until it was powerful enough to carry all kinds of bad things. It was believed that, in many cases, when the Tupilak was finished, an evil spirit would actually have taken possession of it. Again in secret, the magician would put the doll into the sea, with special magic instructions so that it would float to where the enemy was living and bring evil to that person.

However, there was a catch. If the enemy was also strong in magic, they could reverse the Tupilak and send it back, and it would do all the bad things to the magician who had sent it, and their village too. The only way out was for the magician to confess to having made the doll, which would then lose its power.

Below: An eighteenth-century Voodoo ritual of human sacrifice.
Opposite page, top left: African Voodoo fetish.

VOODOO

VOODOO is an African-Caribbean religion with a reputation for using spells and curses. Black Voodoo magic, such as Zombies and Voodoo dolls, have become well known through stories in books and movies—so much so that many people think that's all there is to Voodoo. However, Voodoo is a religion that has both its good and scary sides, but we are looking at the scary side in this book!

LEFT- AND RIGHT-HAND MAGIC

Voodoo has its own witches and wizards. Healing and helpful voodoo magic is called "magic of the right hand," while black or evil Voodoo magic is called "magic of the left hand." Most Voodoo magicians will only do one kind, though a few will work "with both hands."

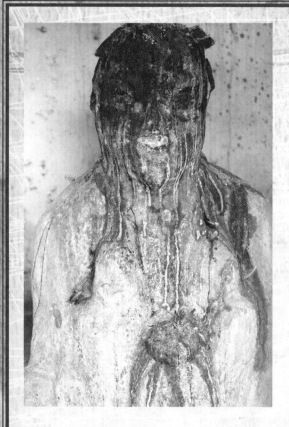

THE VOODOO RELIGION

Voodoo, or vodoun, is a religion combined from a mixture of African beliefs and Roman Catholic Christianity. It began in the days of slavery, but is still practiced today, most commonly in Haiti and in Louisiana, USA. In Voodoo, it is believed that there is one supreme God, but everyday affairs are ruled by the Loa, who are powerful spirits with different areas of responsibility.

ZOMBIE

One very famous part of Voodoo black magic is the use of Zombies (see page 92). These are dead people who are under a spell that makes them walk around and do whatever the magician commands.

VOODOO DOLL

Another famous aspect of Voodoo black magic is the use of dolls. A Voodoo doll or gris-gris can be made to represent your enemy, and you can then stick pins in it, with appropriate spells and curses, to make the enemy suffer.

In fact, you can make a doll for good purposes as well, and can even make a gris-gris of yourself and stick the right kind of pins in to bring yourself good luck—but the bad kind is more frequently used.

The dolls are traditionally made out of sticks bound together with moss and then wrapped in strips of fabric. A face can be stitched onto the fabric.

It may not be necessary even to stick pins in the doll. Marie Laveau, a famous Voodoo magician from New Orleans, used to leave a gris-gris doll on the doorstep of people she wanted to influence. They would be terrified that a hex had been put on them and would come to Marie for guidance on how to get rid of this curse. She would then be able to persuade them to pay her money, or do whatever else she wanted them to do, so that the supposed hex could be lifted.

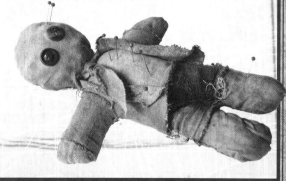

Right: The wicked fairy from *Sleeping Beauty* putting an enchantment on the sleeping baby princess.

POSSESSION

A person or thing is taken over by an unseen force.

A person is said to be "possessed" when it seems that an evil force has taken over their body and is making them do and say bad things against their will. Animals and even objects can also be possessed. There have been numerous well-known cases of possessed people throughout history. However, it's important to remember that, in modern times, many of these supposed "possessions" would now be diagnosed as mental illnesses or conditions such as epilepsy.

EXORCISM

A religious ceremony to rid a place or person of evil influences.

Sometimes a place is being used by a spirit or poltergeist to such an extent that people find it impossible to live there, and something has to be done to make the spirit move on. Most major religions have an established ceremony for exorcism, including prayers and ritual gestures such as sprinkling holy water. A priest will try to communicate with the unwanted spirit, and either persuade it to leave or threaten it with punishment from higher beings if it doesn't go. This usually works. Exorcism can also be tried when a person is believed to be possessed, though good results are less predictable.

ENCHANTMENT

ENCHANTMENTS are strong spells. They are not considered black magic, but they can have dangerous consequences. Enchantments are cast by powerful magicians and enchanters.

FAMOUS ENCHANTMENTS

Many famous fairy tales contain enchantments. In *Sleeping Beauty*, the princess is magically plunged into a deep sleep for 100 years until a prince fights his way through the forest and breaks the spell. In *Beauty and the Beast*, a prince is enchanted and has to live as a monster until someone loves him the way he is, as a monster. This kind of long-term enchantment can be seen as an imprisoning spell—the person is not killed or permanently harmed, but is locked in a magical state until someone else releases them. Often the conditions for ending the enchantment are very difficult, so the chances of rescue are slim. In Hans Christian Andersen's *The Wild Swans*, Elisa's brothers are turned into swans and can only be turned back if she makes shirts for all of them out of stinging nettles. She must also not speak a word, or they will die. Only remarkable courage or selflessness can break this kind of spell.

Left: An eighteenth-century priest carries out an exorcism.

FAMOUS DOPPELGÄNGERS

Queen Elizabeth I of England, when old and ill, saw her Doppelgänger lying on her bed. The Queen refused to go to bed and stood up, sat in a chair, and even lay on the floor for days until she died.

American President Abraham Lincoln saw his Doppelgänger beside him in the mirror several times, looking pale. His wife said she feared that it meant he would not leave office alive. He was assassinated five years later.

DOPPELGÄNGER

THE WORD DOPPELGANGER is German and means "double-walker" or "double-goer." Seeing your own Doppelgänger, or your "shadow self," is bad, and is usually a warning that you are about to die.

Queen Elizabeth I

SHADOW SELF

A Doppelgänger is not the same thing as a "double" or "look-alike," and it is not a ghost either—your Doppelgänger actually is another you or your shadow self.

Sometimes, people's shadow selves have been seen by others, while the people were somewhere else, but it generally means bad things will happen to that person. But more often, seeing the Doppelgänger is associated with death—either it's seen by others as an apparition at the time when the person dies, or the person sees their own Doppelgänger, as a warning that bad luck is on its way, or you will soon die.

In Irish mythology, your shadow self who comes to take you away to the afterlife is called your Fetch.

EVIL EYE

THE EVIL EYE is generally considered to be the power to wish misfortune or death onto somebody, just by looking at them. Sometimes people do it on purpose, but some people are cursed and do it without meaning to.

ENVY AND JEALOUSY

The idea of the Evil Eye is found all over the world. Somebody who is believed to put the Evil Eye onto other people is not necessarily a powerful magician. They're more like a channel for all the envy and jealousy that floats around in the world: their gaze can focus this badness onto someone else.

In many different countries, the way to protect yourself and your belongings against the Evil Eye is to have a protective eye that can send the malevolent gaze right back. So you will often see fishing-boats which have an eye painted on them, to protect the boat, its owner, and the fish.

In Middle Eastern and North African countries, a symbol of a hand with an eye in it is often hung up or worn as a charm or amulet against the Evil Eye. It's called a "hamsa," sometimes known as the Hand of Fatima. The hand is open as if pushing the evil influence away, and the eye, often colored bright blue, looks out from the palm of the hand, ready to meet the envious stare and send it back.

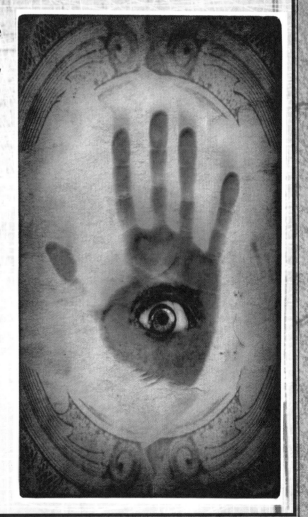

AMULETS AND TALISMANS

AMULETS AND TALISMANS are magical things to wear or carry, which will protect you from evil or bring you luck. Although they have existed since ancient times, people today still like to wear good luck charms. They are thought to ward off evil as well as encourage good things to happen, like good health and long life.

CHARM BRACELETS

These bracelets, which have been popular at different times in history, are simply a collection of small talismans or "lucky charms" attached to a chain. The idea is that the wearer collects, or is given, the charms that she feels will be especially lucky for her.

PROTECTION

The wearing of amulets and talismans has a very long history. In ancient Egypt, most of the jewelry that people wore had a special meaning and most pieces were for protection against bad luck or to bring good things into the wearer's life. A frequently used talisman was the scarab beetle or "khepera," which was associated with the creator god Atum and with the sun. Egyptians were often buried with a khepera amulet over their heart; it was supposed to give protection when their soul would be weighed by the gods to see if it was worthy to enter the afterlife.

In ancient Rome, each child was given a protective amulet, which he or she wore all the time until they grew up. Boys would wear an amulet called a "bulla," while girls wore a moon-shaped pendant called a "lunula."

Traditional amulets in Middle Eastern and Asian countries include the "hamsa" or hand (see page 183) to protect against evil influences, and the

fish which brings fertility and prosperity. Chinese culture has a long tradition of wearing amulets engraved with various symbols such as "double happiness" or the dragon for courage.

MODERN AMULETS AND TALISMANS

In the modern world, many of us still wear or use talismans and amulets, without calling them by those names. People will choose a piece of jewelry connected with their sign of the zodiac, because they believe it will be lucky for them. Many people like to wear the "birthstone" that's considered lucky for people with their birth month—for example, topaz for those born in November. We often also pick our lucky color or lucky number.

A bride is supposed to wear "something old, something new, something borrowed and something blue" to bring her luck on her wedding day and afterwards in her marriage. There are many people who go to an exam or a job interview carrying or wearing something they believe is lucky, whether it's a special coin or pebble, or a handkerchief embroidered with a four-leaved clover, or even a rabbit's foot. We still think of horseshoes as lucky, too.

Top left: Amulet found in the tomb of Egyptian pharaoh King Tutankhamen.
Top right: A pentagram pendant.
Right: Egyptian gold scarab.

INDEX

CREDITS

Images: Every effort has been made to trace and contact the copyright holders prior to publication. If notified, the publisher undertakes to rectify any errors or omissions at the earliest opportunity.

Alamy: 164 t

Art Archive: 69 cr in box, 141 br in box, 142 c front

Art Resource NY: 70 t

Bridgeman Art Library: 4 tl and b, 5 tr, 10 tl, 12 bl in box, 13 b, 14 tr and bl, 15 b, 16–17 t (British Library, London), 16 t front, 17 b front (Haags Gemeentemuseum, The Hague, Netherlands), 18 t, 19 tl and br front, 21 t and br in box, 24 tl, 25 bl in box, 25 br in box, 26 bl, 27 br in box, 28 br in box, 29 tr and bl in box, 30 tr, 31 br in box, 32 tl in box and br in box, 33 t, 38 t, 40 tl in box (Fairy Art Museum, Tokyo, Japan) and br, 41 tl, 42 tl, 44 tr in box, 48 t, 49 br in box, 50 t, 51 cr in box and b, 52 t, 54–55, 56–57 background, 58 cl, 60–61 background, 60 t (Lambeth Palace Library, London), 61 b, 62 t and br in box, 64–65 background, 64 c, 65 br, 66–67 background, 67 tl in box, 68–69 background, 68 t, 70–71 background, 70 br, 71 tl in box and br in box, 72–73 background, 72 t (National Museum, Stockholm, Sweden), 73 tl, 78 tl, 80 br in box, 81 t in box (The Marsden Archive, UK) and bl in box, 82 t, 84 t, 86 tl, 87 br (British Library, London), 88 t and l in box, 89 br in box, 97 tl in box, 106–107 t, 107 b, 110 tl and c, 114 tr in box, 115 t, 116 t, 117 t and bl in box, 125 br, 126 t, 127 tr in box and b (Fairy Art Museum, Tokyo, Japan), 131 t, 133 inset (Canadian War Museum, Ottawa, Canada), 134 b, 134 front, 136 t, 137 bl in box, 138 t, 139 tr in box and b, 143 bl, 144 tl, 147 tr, 154 br, 155 tl, 156 tl in box (British Library, London) and br in box,

159 tl (Staatliche Kunstsammlungen, Dresden, Germany), 162 tl, 165 t and b, 166 b, 167 b, 169 tr in box, 175 tr, 181 t, 182 cr (The National Trust, UK), 184 tr, front cover (4th, 5th and 6th images in strip), back cover (4th, 5th and 6th images in strip)

Corbis: 31 tl, 99 tl in box, br in box, 102 tl, 103 t, 104 br in box, 105 b in box, 107t in box, 112 tl, 117 br, 179 tl in box

Getty Images: 11 br, 12 tr in box, 13 t, 15 t, 20 br, 23 inset, 28 bl in box, 67 br, 74 l and c, 76 cl, 77 br in box, 104 tl in box, 106 cl, 119 inset, 120 tl, 121 bl in box, 122 b in box, 128 br in box, 164 b in box, 178 tl, 180 b, front cover (1st image in strip), back cover (vampire and 1st image in strip)

Granger Collection: 135 br in box, 140 t and cl,

iStockphoto: other images as follows:

butterfly 154; cauldron 25; cross stitches 10, 12, 13, 15, 26, 30, 32, 37, 40, 45, 48, 58, 76, 81, 85, 99, 107, 112, 116, 120, 122, 125, 129, 130, 136, 139, 144, 150, 156, 162, 164, 165, 168, 169, 178; demon 180; evil eye 183; forest 22–23; frames 25, 27, 77, 87, 114, 159; grim reaper 102; grunge borders 11, 13, 17, 27, 31, 49, 59, 61, 65, 67, 71, 82, 88, 111, 112, 121, 130, 135, 141, 163; hands 11, 13, 17, 27, 29, 31, 49, 59, 61, 65, 67, 71, 82, 88, 111, 112, 121, 122, 130, 135, 141, 147, 163; mirror 2, 82, 182; mountain landscape 58–59; owl 158; pentagram 176; ring 177; scratches 36, 37, 38, 39; sphinx 161; stick borders 10, 24, 56, 64, 66, 68, 76, 78, 86, 92, 110, 120, 134, 140, 144, 150, 162, 168; vampire 82; vampire smile 79; voodoo doll 179; werewolf 37

Martin Hargreaves: 6–7, 20 tl, 34 t, 49 t, 53 r, 85 tl, 113 t, 122 t, 129 tr, 143 tr, 146 tl, 152 b, 155 tr, 171 b

Shutterstock: all other images

KEY: t = top, b = bottom, l = left, r = right, c = centre

An Imprint of Sterling Publishing
387 Park Avenue South
New York, NY 10016

SANDY CREEK and the distinctive
Sandy Creek logo are registered
trademarks of Barnes & Noble, Inc.

Copyright © 2012 by Weldon Owen
Limited

This 2013 edition published by Sandy
Creek.

Concept and Project Manager Ariana Klepac
Designer Emilia Toia
Design Assistant Haylee Bruce
Picture Researcher Ariana Klepac
Text Scott Forbes (Forest, Castle, Desert),
Barbara Cox (all other text)
Indexer Trevor Matthews
Production Director Dominic Saraceno
Production and Prepress Tristan Hanks

ISBN 978-1-4351-4971-7

The paper used in the manufacture of this book is
sourced from wood grown in sustainable forests.
It complies with the Environmental Management System
Standard ISO 14001:2004

A WELDON OWEN PRODUCTION
Conceived and produced by Weldon Owen Limited

Printed and bound in China by 1010 Printing Int Ltd.
Lot #:
2 4 6 8 10 9 7 5 3 1
05/13